D1280428

Camp David Diaries

Volume III

MAMIE EISENHOWER
(1953 - 1961)

Copyright © 2002 Sterling-Miller
All rights Reserved

First published by
Sterling-Miller Publishing Co. Inc.
Sterling-Miller Books
12573 Woodmill Drive
Palm Beach Gardens, Florida 33418, U.S.A.

First Printing, April 2002
10 9 8 7 6 5 4 3 2

Printed in the United States

CAUTION: PUBLISHERS NOTE
This is a work of fiction. Names, characters, places, and incidents either are the product of the author's imagination or are used fictitiously.

Without limiting the rights under copyright reserved above, no part of this publication may be reproduced, stored in or introduced into a retrieval system, or transmitted, in any form, or by any means (electronic, mechanical, photocopying, recording, or otherwise), without the prior written permission of both the copyright owner and the above publisher of this book.

Books are available at quantity discounts when used for instructional, educational, promotional or service needs. For information please write to Premium Marketing Division, Sterling-Miller Publishing Co. Inc. 12573 Woodmill Drive, Palm Beach Gardens, Florida 33418.

ISBN: 0-931791-05-7

Library of Congress Control Number: 2002101462

Produced by
Sterling-Miller Books
Palm Beach Gardens, FL
In cooperation with
LegacyWords
Charlottesville, VA

ACKNOWLEDGMENTS

This book would not have been possible without Doris Kearns Goodwin, William Manchester, John van Dalen, Carl Sferrazza Anthony, Dr. David Prensky, Patti Sherman, Geoffrey Perret, J.B. West, Lorraine Sandow, the First Ladies Museum, the Presidential Libraries, and the First Ladies themselves. Most importantly, I lovingly dedicate this project to Dr. Stuart A. Sandow who has been my inspiration.

Camp David Diaries

Book List

		<u>Available</u>
Volume 1	Anna Eleanor Roosevelt Administration 1933 - 1945	11/2001
Volume 2	Elizabeth Wallace Truman Administration 1945 - 1953	02/2002
Volume 3	Mamie Doud Eisenhower Administration 1953 - 1961	04/2002
Volume 4	Jacqueline Bouvier Kennedy Administration 1961 - 1963	05/2002
Volume 5	Lady Bird Johnson Administration 1963 - 1969	08/2002
Volume 6	Pat Ryan Nixon Administration 1969 - 1974	10/2002
Volume 7	Elizabeth Bloomer Ford Administration 1974 - 1977	12/2002
Volume 8	Rosalynn Smith Carter Administration 1977 - 1981	02/2003
Volume 9	Nancy Davis Reagan Administration 1981 - 1989	04/2003
Volume 10	Barbara Pierce Bush Administration 1989 - 1993	06/2003
Volume 11	Hillary Rodham Clinton Administration 1993 - 2001	08/2003

See order form at back

Foreword

Eleanor Roosevelt began the *Camp David Diaries* in 1942. She had been First Lady longer than anyone in history. During her early years, she sought guidance from former First Ladies with little success, so she learned to make her own way in this very difficult job. But Eleanor knew that there must be an easier way. On her first visit to Shangri-La (which is what Camp David was called back then), she found a blank diary in her closet. It seemed pre-destined. She was a prolific writer, and she had a story to tell. She wanted to let future First Ladies learn from her many years of experience in the White House. Following is an excerpt from the very first entry in Eleanor Roosevelt's *Camp David Diary*.

July 18, 1942

I begin this diary with the hope it may act as a primer, if you will, for those of us elected to this special sorority. As First Ladies, we are women with one overriding commonality: a husband who, for a brief moment in history, is the leader of one of the most powerful countries in the world. More importantly, we are women who are individuals in our own right. No matter the strain, we must not loose sight of that.

So often I wish I had someone to tell me how to do this job, give me support and encouragement, someone I could go to for advice. Then I had a thought – why not establish a private, revolving series of handbooks for and by First Ladies? No one knows this role better than those few of us who live it through, why not compile our experiences for those women who follow? So, I begin this first diary and hope that you First Ladies who follow me will continue to add diaries of your own.

I feel that somehow I know you all. I know your strength, your will, your determination and grace. And I know you are brave. None of us (in our right minds!) would choose this life. We get swept in because of our husband's job. We try to be good wives and support our husband's political career over the years. Then one day he gets elected president, and we are expected to successfully handle a position of enormous responsibility for which we did not even apply. It is a job with no handbook, no guidelines, yet one that undergoes constant re-definition of expectations.

It is peaceful here at Shangri-La, away from the overwhelming activities of the White House, and very conducive to this endeavor, at least for the time being. Once this awful war is over, we will no longer need the safety of this retreat. Until then, I will leave the diary here.

I feel strongly that this diary should be kept for our private use. So, each of us must turn over its guardianship to the succeeding First Lady with the utmost of confidentiality.

And so we begin.

Eleanor Roosevelt

Introduction

It just didn't seem right to her that the President and First Lady would be taking a train all the way to Missouri. *Why would they want to do that?* Mamie Eisenhower wondered. She studied Bess Truman as they took the traditional White House tour. *After all they've done for this country, they shouldn't have to go home on the train like ordinary citizens.* But Bess Truman insisted they were ordinary citizens now.

Looking around at her home of seven and one-half years, Bess admitted that it hadn't been such a bad place to live after all. "Once you put your personal touch to the place," she told Mamie, "it really becomes a home."

They continued strolling down the hall of the second floor family quarters. After a few minutes, Bess guided Mamie into her sitting room. "I have a present for you. Shh. It's a secret." Reaching into the drawer of her desk, Bess pulled out a small leather diary that was tied up in a pink satin bow and handed it Mamie. "This one is blank, for you to write in, but there are two more diaries at Shangri-La. One was written by Mrs. Roosevelt, and one by me. I think you'll find them useful."

"Thank you, dear." Mamie slipped the little book into her brown alligator handbag. She wanted to ask a million questions, but Bess was already out the door. As Mamie hurried to catch up, she thought about the strange gift. *Why do they think I'd like to keep a diary? And why do they want me to read their personal diaries? This is all very mysterious.*

Preface

Mamie Eisenhower serves our country as First Lady from 1953 to 1961. This era is known as the Fabulous Fifties. It's a time of prosperity and, for the most part, peace. It is so relatively carefree that President Eisenhower has time to play over 800 games of golf during his eight-year administration. As a matter of fact Ike played so much golf that during his campaign for a second term someone made a bumper sticker that read: "Ben Hogan for President. If we've Got to Have a Golfer in the White House, Let's Have a Good One."

The median family income is $5,600 a year, and a family of four can get along on $60 a week. Shopping centers – the newest phenomena – are being built everywhere. Young couples are making purchases on the installment plan, something that shocks their parents (who had lived through the Great Depression and learned to "make do"). Advertising slogans of the times sum up the carefree mindset of young people: "If I have but one life to live, let me live it as a blonde." "Where there's life – there's Bud." And "See the USA, in Your Chevrolet."

You can buy an Edsel for $4,000. Playboy magazine costs half a dollar, and TV Guide is fifteen cents. Steak is $.92 a pound, milk is 22 cents a quart and bread is 16 cents a pound.

It is the Golden Age of Television: *The Howdy Doody Show, Mickey Mouse Club, Sky King, Ozzie and Harriet, American Bandstand* and *Hopalong Cassidy* keep us mesmerized. But while we all stay home to watch TV, five thousand movie theaters close across the country.

When we do go to the movies, we see: *Rebel Without a Cause, On the Waterfront, High Noon* and *Dial M for Murder*.

We still listen to the radio. Some of our favorite songs are *Standing on the Corner; Come on-a My House; Hey There, You With the Stars in Your Eyes*; and *You Ain't Nothin' But a Hound Dog*. The Fred Waring and Lawrence Welk orchestras keep our toes tapping whether we listen to them on LP's or watch them on television.

The news is announced by John Cameron Swayze and the new team of Huntley and Brinkley. We read a wide range of books: *The Caine Mutiny, Peyton Place, The Catcher in the Rye, Profiles in Courage*, and *The Cat in the Hat*.

The McCarthy Hearings are still in full force, and the polio epidemic cripples more than 50,000 people, mostly children. Fortunately Dr. Jonas Salk is busy working on his vaccine. Our newest social event is the Tupperware Party.

Boys are sporting ducktail haircuts and wearing white T-shirts with a pack of cigarettes rolled up in their sleeves, while men sport a new look in Bermuda shorts. Girls are wearing poodle skirts and saddle shoes. At the beauty shop they can get Mamie bangs or a poodle cut for $2. Teenagers hang out at drive-ins – both the movie kind and the restaurant kind – and children play with Hula Hoops.

During this time we have a new Interstate Highway system; our postal rates for first class stamps increase from three cents to four (the first increase in 24 years); Grace Kelly marries Prince Ranier; Maria Callas begins dating Aristotle Onassis; a young lawyer by the name of Fidel Castro starts a revolution in Cuba; and we add two new states to the union: Alaska and Hawaii.

Well, now that we've had a chance to refresh our memories about what was going on during the Eisenhower administration, there's someone I want you to meet. I hope you enjoy getting to know Mamie Eisenhower through her *Camp David Diary*.

Pamela K. Thorson

Editor's Note

In the original diaries, First Ladies wrote comments in the margins of each other's diaries. As this is difficult to reproduce legibly, we have placed Mamie Eisenhower's diary entries on the right pages, with the corresponding comments of other First Ladies on the left pages.

Camp

David

Dairies

Volume III

MAMIE EISENHOWER
(1953 - 1961)

February 15, 1953

To all future First Ladies,

    This diary is just a peachy idea! What a delightful way to pass along ideas. Though writing doesn't come easily to me, I will record my experiences and lessons as often as I can.

    I am greatly humbled (but also excited) about our new life in the White House. I don't see any reason to run it differently than I have any of our other homes. I'll run it on a strict budget and a tight schedule. Guess I've been "in the military" so long now that it's hard to break old habits.

    I think it is also very important to keep personal expenses separate from the people's money. "Don't run it on the Eagle" is what we used to say in the Army. Ladies, we have a heavy responsibility to the people of this country in the husbandry of their money. I encourage each of you to be prudent.

                           Mamie

President Eisenhower was so organized and thorough and such a good military leader that Jack asked him to come to Camp David to discuss the Cuban problem at the Bay of Pigs. They are outside right now deep in conversation. I can't help but notice the contrast that Jack is the youngest man ever elected president and Mr. Eisenhower is the oldest. It only seems natural that they would confer.

Jackie

Lyndon didn't use Camp David much at first, so he wrote to Ike inviting him and Mamie to use the retreat as often as they would like. They never took up our offer.

Lady Bird

Being at this Camp makes me think about President Eisenhower at lot. Ike never made it back to Camp David. He died yesterday. We are here while Dick prepares the eulogy for his friend.

Pat N.

March 10, 1953

Ike and I are settling in to the routine of the White House. Ike is trying to get this place organized (once a military man, always a military man). For instance, in the past most presidents opened their own mail. That must have taken forever. Ike gets hundreds of pieces of mail a day. Ike has his staff open his mail, remove the letters they can answer, and then he reviews the few remaining pieces.

He also got tired of signing "Dwight D. Eisenhower" all the time. (He told me he wished his name was John Doe or something short like that.) So, he asked the Attorney General if initials were just as legal as a full name, and they are. Since then he has been signing DE or just E.

Ike also found out that he has to sign every presidential pardon that comes across his desk – over a thousand each year. But, he's going to get the law changed so that he can sign one pardon a year with all the names on it. It's much more efficient.

He has two staffs: one for his personal needs and one for the official duties of the presidency. Ike told them he wants each letter or memo to have a one-line or one paragraph synopsis before it is put on his desk. That way he can read the synopsis and decide whether he needs to read the whole paper.

All in all, Ike is trying to whip the West Wing into shape, and it seems to be working. It's not the military, but it's getting better.

Mamie

When the Harrison's moved into the White House, it was badly in need of modernization. They put in electricity for the first time, but Mrs. Harrison was so afraid of what she called the "magic lights," that she wouldn't turn them on or off. She had the servants do it. Sometimes the lights stayed on all night until the staff got to work the next day! By the way, she was very artistic and designed her own set of presidential china.

Jackie

Everything was so beautiful after Jackie finished redecorating that all we brought to the White House was our bedroom furniture. We didn't have to bother with a redecorating budget, thank goodness.

Lady Bird

Jackie purchased the White House crystal from Morgantown, West Virginia. She wanted to have American made craftmanship, but she also wanted to bring attention to the severe poverty of the Appalachian region.

Rosalynn

I also asked the public for donations of money. We received over $700,000 for the redecorating and $200,000 for new White House china (I didn't design it, though). The press tries to make a big deal out of the money I spend, but I don't think the American public minds. They realize that the most powerful country in the world has to look it.

Nancy

When George and I got married during WWII, rationing was a part of our daily life. My mother was very resourceful like Mamie. She went around to all the neighbors and borrowed rationing coupons so that I could have a new pair of shoes for our wedding.

Barbara

During WWI, money was tight and there were also shortages of everything. So to set a good example for the country, Edith Wilson put a flock of sheep on the White House lawn to graze. It reduced the number of men needed on the grounds crew, and they were released so that they could do more productive wartime work. Plus, the wool was sold and the money given to charity.

HRC

April 12, 1953

Trying to run this house on the budget they gave me is almost impossible. Let me give you an example. I was shocked to find out that there was only $375 left in the decorating account for the White House when we moved in. $375! It wasn't because Bess was a spendthrift - quite the contrary. But the Truman's had to do extensive restoration work just to save the White House from falling down, so $375 was all that was left.

The third floor was desperately in need of curtains. So, I went out to Fort Myer and bought up some surplus parachute silk for ten cents a yard. Lillian Parks, the White House seamstress, did them up into curtains, and they look lovely.

Fortunately, bargain hunting is fun for me. I cut coupons from the newspaper and magazines and have the staff use them when shopping. I also call the stores myself and ask to speak with the manager. If you go to the top, you get better deals.

People think my hats are Paris originals, but I get them from mail order for $9.95!

So, I'm sure can manage with this budget. One of the first things I did was ask all Americans to donate antiques and china to furnish the People's Home. A few items have already been sent to us, and they're just beautiful. Army wives know how to be resourceful!

Mamie

The title of First Lady evolved over the first few presidencies. Initially, there was no official title. Martha Washington was called "Lady Washington." (The colonies couldn't quite break with their British titles.) Abigail Adams was called "Lady." Elizabeth Monroe wanted to just be called Mrs. Monroe, but the press referred to her as Queen Elizabeth because she was so elegant. Dolley Madison was addressed as "Lady Presidentress," and Julia Tyler was known as the "Lovely Lady Presidentress." Wow, isn't that ostentatious. The title First Lady was used by President Zachary Taylor during his eulogy for Dolley Madison in 1849. He said, "She was truly our First Lady for a half-century." We've been using the title ever since.

Jackie

Some never had a chance to achieve greatness. Lucretia Garfield was First Lady for just a few months when President Garfield was shot. She stayed by his side attending to him in the White House until he died two months later.

Rosalynn

The Prime Minister of England is a woman - Margaret Thatcher. That means her husband is like a First Lady. When I was planning a conference for all international First Ladies, I didn't know what to do about Mr. Thatcher - should I invite him or not. His assistant graciously told me that it wouldn't be appropriate.

Nancy

Mr. Thatcher is called First Gentleman. If we ever have a female President, I think that would be the best title for her husband.

Barbara

Talk about having greatness thrust upon them, Frances Cleveland was only 21 years old when she married President Cleveland shortly after he was elected. But she excelled at being First Lady. She was pretty and vivacious, spoke fluent German and French, and was an accomplished pianist. Cleveland didn't get re-elected, but four years later, he was elected again and Frances was First Lady a second time! Their daughter Esther was the first child born in the White House. She was a very popular First Lady. We join a long line of gracious and singularly strong women.

HRC

June 8, 1953

      After reading the diaries of my predecessors, I have a much greater appreciation of just who Mrs. Roosevelt and Mrs. Truman were, and are. I can only imagine that the First Ladies before them were just as noble. I am honored to be a member of this special sisterhood.

      I want to take this opportunity to thank Bess and Eleanor, all the First Ladies who went before them, and all of you who follow. I think this quote from Shakespeare was written just for First Ladies:

        Some are born great, some achieve greatness, and some have greatness thrust upon them.

               Mamie

I remember my journalist friends telling me about a battle during the Korean War called Operation Smack, which was observed by many high-ranking military officers and several journalists. It was meant to capture prisoners of war. Unfortunately, there were many UN soldiers killed and nothing was accomplished. The reporters said that the battle seemed to have been staged for the entertainment of the officers. On the other hand, one reporter said that the reason for the failure was that there was a shortage of ammunition. There are always two sides of a story. We are struggling with that in Viet Nam, too.

Lady Bird

For such a short war in terms of years fought, the toll was horrible. There were over 50,000 deaths and 100,000 wounded for the U.S. The South Koreans lost 400,000 people and the North Koreans over 500,000. And for what? Nobody gained anything by this war.

Rosalynn

Actually, that quote was originally said by Abraham Lincoln. Mamie must not have been much of a history buff.

Nancy

July 28, 1953

The armistice was finally signed in Korea two days ago. Ike was determined to get peace. He promised in his campaign that he would go to Korea and he did. Then he spent several months working out this agreement. Things weren't going well for a while. It got so bad earlier this Spring that Ike sent atomic bombs to the area. He threatened that if China didn't settle this war, he would use the weapons. The threat worked, and the Chinese started negotiating.

Everything was going along just fine until Syngman Rhee, the leader of South Korea, became a problem. (And we were fighting for him!) He insisted that Korea not be divided. Well Ike, knowing that the other side wouldn't agree to this, told Mr. Rhee that he would ensure military and economic aid if he would accept the treaty. Otherwise, Ike told him the U.S. would pull out their troops. (Ike can be quite convincing. He knows how this military game is played.)

Needless to say, Mr. Rhee agreed and the armistice was signed. I loved Ike's speech to the nation following the signing of the agreement. The one quote I like best is: "With malice toward none, with charity for all." What a beautiful, diplomatic statement.

Thank God the war is over. Now, maybe, our son John can come home. All of our sons can come home.

Mamie

What I enjoy about being First Lady are the opportunities to help people that I would not have had as a private citizen or even as a Senator's wife. I admired the type of First Lady Eleanor Roosevelt was and try to follow her example. Like her, I enjoy traveling across our country supporting the Great Society Programs Lyndon developed. We truly do live in a Great Society.

Lady Bird

I agree. As First Lady, I am able to travel to Africa, China even the Soviet Union. I lovedbeing a goodwill ambassador for our country. I never would have had the courage or opportunity to do that otherwise.

Pat N.

I try to encourage a more active role for women not only in politics but also in their careers whether inside the home or out. Also, because I am First Lady, I am able to publicly discuss my breast cancer. If I was able to increase awareness of the disease and maybe get women to go for checkups that could save their lives, that's about all I can ask for.

Betty F.

August 12, 1953

I love everything about being First Lady. It's an exciting life. You get to meet so many wonderful people and do so many fascinating things. I love to ride in the back of the limousine and wave to people. I think Americans appreciate being able to see the president and his wife. We should be accessible.

Something else I did was have a small box made for me to stand on. I'm so short that when people go by in a reception line, I'm just swallowed up. Now I can look people in the eye!

I also had the tables rearranged for our banquets. Normally, they are put in a U-shape – with Ike and me facing each other. Well, that just wouldn't do. All people see of me is my back. I'm sure they would rather see my face. So, I had the tables put in the shape of an E. That way, Ike and I can sit next to one another (in grand, high-back chairs) at the top of the E and everyone can see us.

Another thing I love about living in the White House is that Ike is here most of the time. I can reach over and pat his bald head anytime I want to.

Mamie

I think television had a great deal to do with Jack becoming president. Public speaking has always been easy for him, so doing television was not difficult. Mr. Nixon was not comfortable in front of the cameras, so during the debates he did not look convincing no matter what he had to say.

Jackie

On the other hand, I think television was the undoing of Lyndon. There was so much graphic coverage of the Viet Nam war it was kept in the public eye constantly. Lyndon was constantly reacting to situations instead of having time to study and act.

Lady Bird

Yes, Dick was very uncomfortable before the cameras during his debates with Jack Kennedy. But I think he's gotten much better with practice. We didn't bring in anyone like Robert Montgomery, but we had a public relations person give him some advice. TV is important to a politician today.

Pat N.

I think that television - actually all media - has gotten too powerful. They now demand information "because the public has a right to know." Well, the public has no right to know what goes on behind my closed bedroom door any more than I have a right to peek into their bedroom window. These formerly august and noble media companies have turned to tabloid sensationalism. It's disgusting, but we don't seem to be able to do anything about it.

HRC

December 7, 1953

Television has become so important in our lives now. It's hard to believe, but over 30% of the people in America own TV sets today.

Ike has given a few speeches on television, but he is very uncomfortable doing it. Henry Cabot Lodge told him that he needed to be the "TV President," and that television was the best way to get message across to Americans. Henry told him it would be good for his popularity and would help to get his legislative programs passed. If more Americans knew about them, they could pressure their own legislators.

But Ike was concerned because he struggles so with his televised speeches. He hates the teleprompter. It's always going too fast or jumping ahead. Anyway, Edward R. Murrow advised Ike to get help, so he called Robert Montgomery — one of our favorite movie stars.

Mr. Montgomery made Ike rehearse his speeches over and over; he showed him how to wear makeup (I still giggle about that!), suggested he wear blue shirts instead of white and told his barber to let his hair grow on the sides. Ike drew the line at his hair; he wanted a GI cut as usual.

The television cameras and the crew made Ike nervous, so Mr. Montgomery had them hidden behind black cloths with only the lens sticking out. It seems to have finally worked. Ike gave a speech the other night in the Oval Office, but instead of just sitting there, he got up and walked around a little. He felt more comfortable, and looked it.

Mamie

All this entertaining requires a huge wardrobe for the women in our family (including daughters-in-law). It just so happens we are all about the same size, so we pooled our clothes and set up a room on the second floor (we call it the gown room). I didn't mind buying clothes so much when I know others can wear them, too. I also decided that I can't be dressed perfectly all the time. I was putting too much tension on myself. So, I relaxed and made myself at home.

Rosalynn

$17.95 for a dress seems practically impossible - even if it was 30 years ago. I don't think she had very many dresses that cost that little. Despite Mamie's claim that she didn't buy a lot of clothes, I happen to know that she had Mrs. Truman's bedroom turned into her dressing room. It was filled with racks and racks of dresses, as was a room on the third floor. She was quite a clothes horse. I pale by comparison.

Nancy

I love nice clothes, but I'm not much of a shopper. As a matter of fact, I bought my wedding dress at the very last minute. I raced into a department store in Fayetteville just before closing and bought a dress right off the rack. It just didn't seem important to me. Bill and I had been living together for several years; the wedding ceremony was really just a show for our families and for his political future.

HRC

February 16, 1954

Well, I'll be. I was just notified that I've been named to the New York Dress Institute's list of the world's twelve best-dressed women!

It certainly came as a surprise to me. I don't spend money foolishly on clothing. I mostly order my everyday dresses from catalogs, and they cost about $17.95 each. But I do know the difference between pinching pennies and spending them. I like to look nice without breaking the bank. And my gowns are by American designers. Nettie Rosenstein designed the beautiful one I wore to Ike's inauguration. Mostly, I like dresses designed by Molly Parnis, and I love Sally Victor hats.

I buy clothes that I can get good wear out of. I don't think it's sensible to buy something just because it's in style that season, and then never wear it again. I think First Ladies just have to have common sense and know fashion from fad.

Mamie

I dictate thank you notes into my tape recorder. That way I can do my notes any time of the day or night or while I'm traveling, and the secretaries can transcribe them during the workday.

Lady Bird

One of the most important projects I did in the White House was to make it more accessible for people with handicaps.

Pat N.

We still send all the flowers to charities. I'm glad to know who started the tradition.

HRC

April 9, 1954

I thought I'd throw in a few practical pieces of advice. I know that's what Mrs. Roosevelt wanted us to do.

For one thing, we have so many flowers at state dinners; I just couldn't stand the thought of throwing them away. So now, after the dinners, I send all the flowers to local hospitals. It cheers up the patients and is not so wasteful.

It's also important to answer every piece of mail. I've been getting between 750 and 1,000 pieces a month. I respond to every one of them. I believe if someone takes the time to write, they deserve a proper answer. Mostly I dictate to my secretary Mary Jane McCafree. She types them up and I sign them. But sometimes, I like to personally write a note. Especially thank yous. A thank you note is extremely important - don't forget them.

I write so many notes that Senator Stuart Symington once said to me: "You always write as if you mean it. I suppose that is one of the reasons you have the country in the palm of your hand." I don't know about that, but I know it's important.

There are lots of people who want me to help with charities and so forth. I try to help as much as I can. I think it's just good neighborliness. I help with

I know that Florence Harding was extremely kind to her servants and staff. She regularly had garden parties for them and for wounded WWI vets.

Jackie

money when I can, but other times it's a helping hand. Once a blind musician sent me a piece of music he'd written. It was lovely, so I arranged an audition for him with the National Symphony Orchestra. As long as I am in this position, and people listen to me, I want to help as many citizens as I can. No sense having all this power and not use it!

Finally, I think it is important to treat the household staff well. A simple thank you, a birthday cake, a get well card are all much appreciated by them. I know everyone's name and try to find out as much about their families as possible. If they're sick, I send flowers. And I give each one a cake and present on their birthday.

It is important for the servants to know who's boss, but a thoughtful boss makes everything more enjoyable.

Mamie

The major enhancement to Camp David since Lyndon became President is telephone capacity. Twenty-five new long-distance phone lines were added this month between here and Thurmont. Lyndon has so many meetings that it was necessary for our communications as well as the press.

Lady Bird

The first day we arrived, we noticed that the "Camp David" sign had been taken down. In its place was a sign that read "Camp #3." Dick was angry and immediately ordered the original sign located and hung back up. Because Dick admired Ike so much, it was important to him that the name Ike gave the camp be displayed.

Pat N.

We had to repair Aspen, Hickory and Maple because of moisture and termite damage. The dispensary was in such bad shape that it had to be torn down and another one built. We also had to re-do the steam heating system that Bess and Harry put in almost 30 years ago. We were going to put in solar heating panels, but there isn't enough sunlight in these dense woods, so instead we added wood-burning stoves to several of the cabins, including ours.

Rosalynn

May 1, 1954

There have been many much needed changes to the camp, not the least of which is the name. Ike felt (and I must say I agreed) that the name "Shangri-La" was just a little too fancy for an old soldier. After much discussion (I wanted to name it Camp Catoctin, after the mountains), Ike prevailed with Camp David, named after our dear little grandson. I think it is much too personal. I tried to talk him out of it, but when the General makes up his mind, he usually gets his way. The name will probably change with each new president anyway. I'm surprised that the Trumans left the name as it was with Bess being so unassuming. But they didn't come out here very often, so I suppose they just didn't bother.

All of the cabins have been renamed, too. I won that battle and was allowed to select the names. I named them after trees, with the main house where we live called "Aspen." So much better than calling it the Bear's Den!

We have greatly modernized everything, and the place is much improved. I no longer feel like I'm at a hunting lodge. We painted many of the interior walls to brighten up the cabins (pink and green with beige accents in our bedroom, as usual). I always decorate our bedroom with the same colors. After living in dozens of homes over the past 36 years or so, it gives us a little continuity - it gives us a sense of "home." I think that is so important.

Dick likes to use the BBQ grill when we are out here, and the girls love having cookouts with their friends. I haven't done much redecorating at the White House, but we did make Camp David more to our liking. There wasn't much of a budget, so we had to get funding from wherever we could - even from private citizens, like Mamie did at the White House. Except we had the public give money instead of furnishings. Dick said that if the money was given to the Navy, it could be spent however we wanted without the appropriations committee or anyone like that involved. One of Dick's supporters donated enough money for the new tennis courts. We also increased the operating budget for Camp David from $148,000 a year to $640,000, which helps tremendously.

Pat N.

We tore out the beaverboard ceiling in the living room and discovered a much higher ceiling with exposed beams above it. We replaced the east wall with windows, which let in a lot of daylight.

We also added an outdoor cooking and eating area. It will be such fun when the family comes out.

By the way, I got rid of that horrible wagon wheel chandelier that hung in the living room. Can't imagine either Mrs. Roosevelt or Bess allowing such a thing in her home!

Mamie

We prefer watching movies to television. Jack even had the Navy men take movies of us doing different things at Camp David. One is of Caroline riding her pony, one is of me skeet shooting (I'm not very good!), and there is a cute one of John playing with his dog. They put music with the movies, and they are wonderful fun. We watch them over and over.

Jackie

My favorite show is "Gunsmoke." I was in love with James Arness (who plays Marshal Dillon) until I found out he was a Republican. How could he? Lyndon watches three televisions at once, but he only watches the news programs.

Lady Bird

The sailors and marines like to watch movies so they brought a videocassette recorder to Camp David for their cabin. I don't like the machine. I think movies look better on film than on those new cassette tapes. Ronnie and I prefer to use the movie projector.

Nancy

Our grandchildren use the VCR all the time up here. (I know that the Reagans did, too, toward the end of their administration.) The children also love playing their Nintendo games. It's amazing the changes there have been. My family used to sit around listening to radio programs like "The Shadow." We were fascinated. Nowadays, kids can't sit still for a minute.

Barbara

June 19, 1954

We had a television set installed at Camp David. I sure do enjoy watching television – I suppose because it's so new and all. Ike and I watch TV while we eat dinner. Since we like to watch different programs, we had two of the round screens put into the wall in our sitting room at the White House. That way Ike can watch his Westerns, and I can watch "I've Got a Secret," or "What's My Line."

My favorite show is "I Love Lucy." I like it so much that I invited the cast to come to the White House last year. (I don't care if Lucille Ball _is_ on Senator McCarthy's list of suspected communists!) We had a great time.

The most exciting thing of all was that they included me in one of their episodes. It was about how neither Lucy nor I liked to play golf.

That Lucy is always getting into trouble! She leads the kind of life I wish I had lived. So carefree, fun and just plain silly. It's hard for a general's wife to be silly – and impossible for a president's wife!

Mamie

When the debate to censure Senator McCarthy was taking place, Jack was in the hospital with horrible back pain. He didn't have to vote, and maybe that was a good thing. Jack's father was a friend and contributor to Senator McCarthy. His sister Eunice even dated McCarthy for a while. Jack said he probably wouldn't have voted to censure, so I guess that saved him later embarrassment.

Jackie

I was always uncomfortable with Dick's friendship with Joe McCarthy. But I couldn't say anything.

Pat N.

June 20, 1954

This month the Senate came up with a resolution to censure Joe McCarthy. However, as head of the Senate and a close friend of McCarthy's, Dick Nixon had the language in the resolution exclude the word censure. It made the resolution weaker, but the result was the same. McCarthy's hearings are over! It's been such a long, horrible ordeal.

Ike and I are not friends of his. As a matter of fact, we had a dinner last fall and invited all of the Senators and their wives except McCarthy. We didn't want that man in our home.

Ike's favorite thing to say now is: "Have you heard the latest? McCarthyism is McCarthywasm."

Mamie

All of our husbands will have to make very hard decisions as President. It seems such a very difficult road. The CIA made many mistakes before and during the Bay of Pigs invasion, but Jack as Commander-in-Chief had to accept responsibility for everything.

Jackie

I remember reading in the newspaper about a picket sign that read: Two Fried Rosenbergers Coming Right Up. What a disconcerting moment in history.

Lady Bird

Lyndon struggles daily with decisions he has to make about the fighting in Viet Nam. I watch helplessly as it tears him apart. I don't know what to do.

Lady Bird

Jimmy has had to make decisions that are very unpopular. His boycott of the Olympic Games was very difficult. He also is convinced that he is right not to give in to the terrorists that are holding the hostages in Iran. We will not light the White House Christmas tree or attend any public celebrations until the hostages are freed. The boycott and the dark tree are symbols of Jimmy's commitment to this country.

Rosalynn

June 24, 1954

There were demonstrations and pickets outside of the White House most of last week. On the 19th, Julius and Ethel Rosenberg were executed for treason. Some of the demonstrators were against capital punishment, and the rest felt justice was being served.

I'm really torn up about it. On one hand, I love this country and don't want to have anything to do with radicals and communists. But, on the other hand, I think killing someone is wrong, too.

I suppose every administration has these kinds of dilemmas to handle. Before Ike was elected, I used to read about events a President was taking care of, form my own opinions (sometimes pretty strong ones!) then criticize or agree with the resulting decisions. I guess I was judging people and their actions without knowing the whole truth.

Now that Ike is the one in power, and the one who has to make those awful decisions, I see how difficult it truly is. Everything has to be weighed so that truth and justice are served. Sometimes you have to make a decision that is against your better judgment or even your beliefs. But in this role, decisions must be made for the better good of all. I know that sometimes Ike even has to make "deals" with Senators or Congressman in order to get a bill passed. He hates doing that, but he has come to realize that's how the game in Washington is played.

Mamie

This month, Mr. Churchill was made an honorary American Citizen. Jack was so pleased to be able to sign that declaration.
                                        Jackie

Sir Winston Churchill died on January 24th at the age of 90. He was given a state funeral at St. Paul's Cathedral, which is quite unusual for a commoner.
                                        Lady Bird

Ike had the Rose Garden ripped up to put a putting green in at the White House.
                                        Jackie

Dick had the putting green at the White House removed. He planted sod on top of it.   Pat N.

Jerry finds the Camp David course frustrating because it's so tiny. But he's not much of a golfer, so I don't know why he complains. He's so bad that Bob Hope has a new career of one-liners: "Jerry Ford is the most dangerous driver since Ben Hur." "One of my most prized possessions is the Purple Heart I received for all the golf I've played with him." "You can recognize him on the course because his golf cart has a red cross painted on top." "The Russians say if we're really serious about disarmament, we'd dismantle his golf clubs."
                                        Betty F.

Bill put a new green on top of Ike's old one at the White House. He uses it a lot when he's mulling things over in his mind.
                                        HRC

July 5, 1954

What a relief it is to get away from Washington. It's much cooler here, of course, but we are also glad to be away from Mr. Churchill. He and Ike have been meeting at the White House all week about the mess in Korea, among other things.

Prime Minister Churchill appears quite old and frail now. So different from the dynamic man we knew him to be just 10 years ago during the height of the War. At dinner last week, we would be in the middle of a polite conversation, and he would drift off and start talking about the cost of bread or his days in chambers...none of it makes a whit of sense. I am almost sorry for him, except he is still uses salty language and is vile in his personal habits. (I think he must have chewed on that same cigar for the last 10 years!)

Our dear friends, the Alton Jones' and the Ellis Slaters, are here with us this weekend. The men have been playing golf at Ike's new three-hole golf course on the grounds. I suspect there is more interest in making bets than on the exercise, though. On the other hand, we women have put the time to much better use playing scrabble and bolivia!

I think this camp ought to be used to entertain friends not just dignitaries. I heard Walter Winchell say once "A real friend is one who walks in when the rest of the world walks out."

Mamie

My very first visit to the White House was to attend a luncheon for Senate wives that Mrs. Eisenhower hosted. The food was not very good, but Mamie was so gracious she made everybody feel at home. It was during this first visit that I noticed how dingy everything looked at the White House, with imitation furnishings and reproductions. The oldest household article couldn't have been more than 10 years old. That must have been a hint of things to come for me.

Jackie

I also remember attending several of these luncheons, but not this one in particular. The women played canasta at most of them. I just wasn't one of the "club" set. I spent my time being a suburban housewife with small children to run from school to doctor's appointments to Cub Scouts. I didn't have time to develop my "social graces."

Betty F.

August 20, 1954

     I had some of the congressional wives out here today for luncheon and canasta. I invite these women to teas and luncheons without regard to whether they are Republicans or Democrats. I usually don't even know which they are, and I don't want to know. I like the person for what they are, my guest.

     What good fun we all had today, except one of the ladies, Mrs. Gerald Ford didn't know how to play canasta, and so she sat on the sofa reading. Pretty young thing, but too quiet for a politician's wife.

     The talk at the tables centered on our husbands and their jobs. We laughed about how they secretly must enjoy the battle.

     Basically, I've always felt that men should run things at the office and women run them at home. Ike runs the country, I turn the pork chops. But when your home is the White House, the distinction can be blurred.

     Like little Betty Ford, I was shy once. But I listened and learned. So ladies, get involved. Not necessarily as much as Mrs. Roosevelt, but do much as you can in your daily life. Get involved in causes. Volunteer or do things for charity. It sets a good example for the nation.

     Most importantly, pay attention to what is going on around you so that you can help your husband. Ultimately, there is only one person he can truly trust, and that's you.

                             Mamie

We are finally building a home of our own, too. It is just outside of Middleburg, Virginia. We've named the homestead "Wexford," after Jack's family county in Ireland. While the house is being built, we are spending more time here at Camp David. I'm so glad we are. It is peaceful and relaxing. I love being able to ride my horses.

Jackie

October 4, 1954

For the first time in our married life, Ike and I are buying a home. Imagine, after 38 years of marriage, this will be the first house we have ever owned.

Actually we have been remodeling a farmhouse near Gettysburg, Pennsylvania. It's for our retirement. I long to sit on the sun porch with my man by my side watching the grass grow. It will be heaven.

Ike wanted to wait another year or two to begin the work in case he doesn't run for re-election. Then it would give him something to do, he says. But I carried on so, the way every woman does when she wants to get her way, that Ike gave in. And now the work is finished.

It seems like it took forever. The carpenters had to come all the way up from Washington and Baltimore. They say the job was made harder because I kept changing my mind. Well, I just couldn't think of everything at once. Looking at blueprints just doesn't mean anything to me, no matter how much it is explained. But once I could actually see the windows in the bedroom, it was obvious they were too small. So they had to be changed. I want to be able to look out over the fields from my bed! And the living room was just the wrong dimensions for our furniture. I don't know why they complained; they only had to move the fireplace once. I didn't ask them to tear down very many walls...although I do wish the kitchen were a little larger.

It took the staff a week to pack and move all of the Kennedy family furnishings and put them into storage. Mrs. Kennedy left a priceless Monet painting for the White House in memory of her husband. We hung it in the Green Room, which was his favorite room. She also asked the staff to put a plaque in the Lincoln Bedroom. It reads: "In this room lived John Fitzgerald Kennedy with his wife, Jacqueline – during the two years ten months and two days he was President of the United States – January 20, 1961 – November 22, 1963." Every time I see it I'm touched by the sentimentality.

Lady Bird

Lady Bird was so gracious after Dick was elected, but before he took office. She let me come to the White House several times to measure and decide what furniture we were going to need. We were able to move in on Inauguration Day without a hitch. Lady Bird even invited our family, the Agnews and the Humphreys to the White House the morning of the Inauguration for breakfast.

Pat N.

One of the strange things about living in the White House is that very little of the furniture is yours. We brought some of our bedroom furniture, but the rest went into storage. Everything is so unfamiliar.

HRC

I also decided to put in what they call centralized air conditioning. We have it at the White House now. The Trumans put it in when they did the renovations. Doesn't that sound high falootin? Well, we're going to live here for many years, so we might just as well be comfortable.

And we were able to finally get all of our furniture out of storage. I haven't seen it for over ten years. It fits just perfectly in our little farmhouse.

We had an open house party for everyone who worked on the remodeling (carpenters and plumbers) and all of our White House domestic staff (the housemaids, butlers, telephone operators and so on). It only seems right that the people who surround us in our daily life – our official family – should share the joy of our first home with us.

Mamie

I remember that during dinner, Dick spilled chili on his white shirt. Mrs. Wilson and Mamie got some soda water and tried to get the stain out. It was interesting to see these two First Ladies acting so ordinary. They did a pretty good job, too, as I recall.

Pat N.

At Jack's Inauguration we had the largest gathering of First Ladies ever. There was Mrs. Eisenhower, Mrs. Wilson, Mrs. Roosevelt, Mrs. Truman, and me, of course.

Jackie

We had an even larger group of First Ladies at a banquet a couple of weeks ago. There were six of us: Lady Bird, Betty, Rosalynn, Nancy, Barbara and me. I told them how much I appreciated their diaries and how important they were to me. We would have been seven, but Jackie was ill. She passed away a week later.

HRC

November 1, 1954

   We had a dinner recently for Vice President and Mrs. Nixon. There was nothing especially significant about the occasion, just an appreciation. I invited both Grace Coolidge and Edith Wilson to join us, but Grace was not feeling well, so just Edith came.

   I have gotten to know Edith Wilson quite well since we took office. She, my mother and I love to have lunch and play bridge together – which we do often. As a matter of fact, just last week Edith came for lunch. She was going on and on about her new Buick. It is black, big like a limousine and she feels elegant driving it. She invited me to ride along to Virginia with her because she was going to speak at a girl's school there, but the Secret Service wouldn't hear of it.

   Edith also told us about the new RCA Victor television set she just bought. She likes to keep up with current events and takes great pleasure in debating about the McCarthy Hearings and the censure (but not to me because I don't like to talk about it).

   I think something should be done to financially help former First Ladies. Edith tells me the only support she gets from the government is franking privileges. That hardly seems fair. I'm going to speak to Ike about it.

                                        Mamie

Camp David is one of the few places I don't have to worry about who's going to see me smoking a cigarette. It seems like such a small pleasure.

Jackie

I, too, like smoking whenever I want to out here. It's a relief not to be so formal. I wear slacks and sweaters while we are here, but Dick is almost always in a shirt and tie. He never seems to relax.

Pat N.

I find that Camp David is the perfect place to recuperate from my breast cancer surgery. It's quiet and the staff is so caring. I got a big welcome home from them today with hugs and kisses all around. Normally the food here is wonderful (and I have the pounds to prove it), but for now I'm on a diet of special foods recommended by the doctor. Tonight I had liver and onions — ick. But I did get Cook to sneak me a piece of chocolate cake!

Betty F.

The dress code for us is blue jeans, flannel shirts and boots. (I enjoy the freedom to smoke cigarettes out here, too. No media around to get it on film.)

Nancy

I like the ideas Mamie had to keep the romance fresh. I don't know that I'll sit on the floor in the Oval Office and eat lunch, but dancing under the stars sounds good. George and I hold hands whenever possible. It keeps us physically and emotionally close — as we've always been. I don't think we should have to change how we act around each other just because our address is 1600 Pennsylvania Avenue.

Barbara

February 3, 1955

One of the things I love most about being at Camp David is that I don't have to do my hair if I don't want to, or get dressed up. I couldn't get away with that at the White House! It's wonderful to sit around all day in my bathrobe and hair curlers. And I can smoke a cigarette any ol' time I want to.

Sometimes Ike is so fretful out here. He paces around chewing on the problems back in Washington. But not me. I am able to completely put that out of my mind when I'm here and relax. So much so that I am fearful one day I won't be able to force myself to go back to Washington!

Never, never, never forget how to relax. Not just out here, but at the White House, too. Set aside a part of each day to spend private time with your husband. He needs it, too. Send him a little love note in the middle of the day. Have a picnic on the carpet in the oval office. Take him dancing on the balcony under the stars. Do little things that break the routine. I'm just learning all of this myself. During Ike's military career, he was away more that we were together. But now that we live "above the shop," we see each other every day. I want to keep our romance fresh. It's fun! Try it!

Mamie

Mamie was always so self-conscious about her disease. She couldn't fly in an airplane for long distances, so sometimes her daughter-in-law or I went in her place. Although I could never take her place, I tried to represent the country like I knew she would. When Dick and I went to South America, there were many anti-American demonstrations. In the car I was riding, a window was broken by rocks. It was quite frightening, but I had to remain calm. I had to be bigger than they were because I knew Mamie would have been gracious in the face of these hooligans.

Pat N.

In all the years I knew Mamie, I had no idea she suffered from Menieres. She sure kept it quiet. I never saw her stumble or appear "tipsy," but I did read about it in the newspapers. I wasn't really sure if I believed it or not. It's good to know the truth.

Betty F.

May 22, 1955

Oh, dear! I just can't get over what the press says about me. They think that I drink too much. It's completely untrue. I remember the first time I stumbled in front of a bunch of reporters. The next day it was "speculated" in the newspapers that I was tipsy.

They also found out that I stay in bed until noon...and that just made all the Olivetti-Underwoods clatter with reports of hangovers - and laziness!

Well, phooey. I think every woman over the age of 50 should stay in bed 'til noon.

The truth is I have Meniere's syndrome. It's an inner ear condition that affects my balance. It causes vertigo. I never know when it's going to hit me. I can be walking down a hall and then all of a sudden hit the wall. I'm all black and blue just from walking around the house!

Vincent Van Gogh suffered from Meniere's - did you know that? He had constant ringing in his ears, like I do - and look what he did to try and stop it! I don't think I'll get that carried away.

On top of it all...I have asthma and a heart condition that the doctors tell me is serious. My legs swell up and are painful if I am on them too much. I don't want to make a big fuss about it, so that's why I handle some of my duties from bed until midday. It's not because I'm inebriated or lazy. I need to keep my feet elevated as much as possible so I can perform my duties as White House hostess.

What a sweet thing for her to say about me. I'm very touched. It's so nice to have her as an in-law since Julie married David. Our families have been together for a long time. I knew that there was talk about removing Dick from the Eisenhower ticket, but I don't think it was personal. There are always political reasons for these things.

Pat N.

From time to time, because of my illnesses, I am not able to attend functions required of the First Lady. So, I send the Second Lady, Pat Nixon. She has been such a helpmate to me; I call her my rock of Gibraltar. Pat presents herself admirably, she's so pretty and genuine, and I never hesitate to ask her.

Not only is Pat wonderful, but Dick has proven to be quite loyal, too. Ike is very lucky to have a vice president like Dick Nixon. He never takes the limelight from Ike, and he works very hard.

Both Ike and his brother Milton are already talking about getting rid of Dick in the next election. But I'll talk them out of it. You can bet your boots on that!

Mamie

Jack and I are young, so I seldom think about our mortality. However, I understand how Mamie felt losing a son. When our little Patrick died, I was inconsolable. I have been pregnant with five babies and only two have lived. God willing, we will have more children. I know our hold on life is fragile, but I just don't dwell on the inevitability. I can't or it will overwhelm me.
Jackie

When we lost our daughter Robin to leukemia, I felt as if part of me died, too. I don't think you ever recover from losing a child.
Barbara

I am so grateful for my healthy child.
HRC

July 29, 1955

My sister-in-law Helen Eisenhower (Milton's wife) passed away on the 20th. She died of cancer. The tragedy is added to by the fact she wasn't even 50 years old.

It scares me to think I might lose Ike before his time. We lost little Ikky, our first son, when he was just three years old. I was only 24 at the time and had already lost all four of my grandparents, two sisters, and my firstborn son. But while these deaths were agonizing to me, I still had my whole life in front of me. Now I don't.

I've thought a lot about my own mortality since Helen died — can't seem to get it out of my mind. It has made me realize just how fragile our hold on this life is. I certainly am looking at things a lot differently now. I hold my grandchildren a little tighter and my husband a little longer. I've come to the conclusion that it's very important to embrace every day with joy and never take anyone for granted.

Mamie

Later the same year as General Eisenhower's heart attack, Jack had surgery on his spine. It was very risky. I kept busy answering all of the cards and letters that came. I was amazed at how important these get-well wishes were to Jack's recovery.

                                                    Jackie

Lyndon had a serious heart attack about the same time Ike did. He had just taken over as Senate majority leader. I took a room next to Lyndon's at Bethesda Naval Hospital, and the first thing I did was set up an office there. That way I could keep an eye on his work and help him. His staff was constantly in and out. At first I was afraid that being majority leader would be too much for him, but the doctors and I agreed that keeping busy could be good for Lyndon.

                                                    Lady Bird

When Ronnie was shot, I decided not to stay with him in the hospital. I didn't want to give the impression to the world that the President of the United States was in critical condition. Even though he was, I just thought it best that everyone felt the country was still in good hands.

                                                    Nancy

September 28, 1955

On September 24th, I, Mamie Doud Eisenhower, saved the life of the President of the United States – my husband. I still can't believe Ike has had a heart attack. As I write this, I'm staying in a room next to his at Fitzsimmons Hospital. Our life has turned upside down.

We were visiting my mother in Denver. Ike came across the hall to my room about two in the morning, and told me his chest hurt. We both thought it was indigestion. He always eats such terrible foods: sausages, onions, sauerkraut and the like! So I gave him some Milk of Magnesia as usual, but this time it didn't seem to help. I got worried and called Howard Snyder, Ike's personal physician, who was staying at a hotel just a few blocks away.

Howard arrived quickly, and I told him that we thought it was just an old fashioned case of indigestion, but he could easily see it was more than that. Ike was in a great deal of pain. He ordered the aide to bring the oxygen canister from his room down the hall. He was out the door and back again before I even noticed.

Howard concentrated on his patient. I can still hear the first words he spoke to Ike: "Now listen here, General, you may be having a heart attack." It took me by surprise. And sure enough, Ike had frightfully high pulse and blood pressure rates. Howard gave Ike several types of medicines to help with the pain and to thin the blood, and then he tried to put an oxygen mask on Ike.

Ike's health was always reported by the press, but no one knew anything about Mamie's health problems. About two years after Ike's heart attack, Mamie had a hysterectomy. It was kept quiet. That wouldn't happen today. Even the most private details about the President and First Lady are made public.

HRC

Well, Ike wouldn't have any of that and kept pushing the mask away from his face.

Howard knew Ike was too unstable to be transported to the hospital right then. He had to get Ike calmed down. If only they could keep him alive until morning, the ambulance ride wouldn't be so dangerous.

Then Howard became concerned about Ike's falling body temperature, which could throw him into shock if it got too low. He packed hot water bottles around Ike's body, while the aide massaged his arms and legs with rubbing alcohol. But all was for naught, and Ike indeed went into shock.

I was frantic with worry, but couldn't seem to do anything about the situation. I watched everything unfold in front of me like a bad dream. My body felt heavy, my mind was screaming questions but nothing came out of my mouth. Pretty soon Howard started to get very worried and told me that we needed to get Ike to the hospital right then, no matter the risk.

But a sudden a calm came over me, and I knew exactly what needed to be done. I threw of all the water bottles off Ike's bed and climbed in with him.

I remember my mother telling me once that the best way to cure a baby of colic was for the mother to lie down on her back, put the baby on her stomach, skin to skin, and let the warmth of her body pull the gas right out. It always worked for my son, why not for my husband?

I always used hot water bottles when my kids had colic. I never heard of this remedy, but it accomplishes the same thing — and it's much more loving. I'll pass this tip along to my children for their children.

Barbara

Mamie kept herself busy all right. She personally answered over 11,000 get-well cards. She kept Ike's spirits up by being cheerful every day and by reading some of the messages to him. And she called the White House almost every day to report on his progress. It's how Dick and I stayed informed. No one else said much to us.

Pat N.

So, I snuggled up to Ike's back – like spooning – and wrapped my body around his. I stroked his arms and even hummed a little lullaby. It seemed to have a soothing effect on Ike, and I felt him relax in my arms. Pretty soon he drifted off to sleep and out of danger. We were able to wait and take him to the hospital the next morning.

Even though he's doing much better, I'm frightened. I don't know what I'd do without Ike. I'm trying to keep myself busy so that I don't have to think about it.

Mamie

I'm so pleased that Mamie was concerned about Dick. I can tell you that he did feel under-appreciated. No one told him he did a good job, and I think that ate away at him.

Pat N.

November 21, 1955

This is our first trip out to Camp David since Ike took ill. There was a National Security council meeting here today and tomorrow is a Cabinet meeting. There are fewer people and interruptions here than at the White House, so we thought this would be the best place to let him get back to work.

Last night, John Foster Dulles (Secretary of State), Charles Wilson (Defense), George Humphries (Treasury) and Ike had a rousing bridge game. But the men kept a wary eye on Ike all night, to make sure he was ok. After all, it's only been two months since the heart attack.

I think Ike is just fine. It's Vice President Nixon I'm worried about. He virtually ran the country during Ike's hospitalization, and did a good job. But now the rooster is back in the hen house, and I think Dick feels awkward. And I'm not sure I blame him. I have never heard anyone give him as much as a "thank you." That could be devastating to a person. I'd hate to see Dick become bitter. He is a very proud man, but I think he needs to hear a word of appreciation from time to time.

And that should be a lesson to all of us: Kind words never die.

Mamie

Even though Jack's father Joe suffered a stroke earlier this year and is now in a wheelchair, the Ambassador is still the head of the Kennedy family. Family must take care of their own.

Jackie

I don't think it's necessarily the right thing for all families to care for their ill or aging relatives. My mother is quite frail now and has been moved to a nursing facility. I don't believe we have abandoned her. She is getting wonderful care - Ronnie and I couldn't possibly care for her any better. I call her every day.

Nancy

General Eisenhower died on the 28th. He had been at Walter Reed Hospital for nine months – with Mamie in a room next to his. She never left his side.

Lady Bird

January 6, 1956

I just had the biggest surprise. Ike gave me a gift after dinner last night. It is a gold pendant necklace that he got at Tiffany's. The inscription says: "For never failing help, since 1916, in calm and in crisis, in dark days and in bright. Love, Ike."

What a lovely sentiment. He told me it was because I've always taken such good care of him, especially after the heart attack. Well, I was brought up to think that if someone you love is ill, it is your job to take care of him. When my grandparents were feeble, my mother took them in. Now we take care of my mother. So when Ike was ill, I just took over. I can't imagine doing it any other way.

We were at the hospital for about seven weeks. I stayed by his side and tried to make him comfortable. My job now is to watch what he eats and make sure he doesn't get too excited about anything. The first thing he was told he couldn't do was watch the Army-Navy football game!

I will have to stay vigilant, but it's worth it. Ike is my life.

Mamie

Our grandson Lyn is the apple of his grandfather's eye.
Lyndon seems to forget all his problems when Lyn is in the room.
I can't get over the transformation. This little boy will keep
Lyndon young. How different the house is when Lyn is here.
Luci and Lyn are staying with us while Pat is in Viet Nam.
Having the Secret Service men watching over our daughter
and grandson makes us feel more at ease.

Lady Bird

We have two grandsons that give us joy. Chip and his wife
and son (Digger) have been living here in the White House since
Digger was born. Sadly, they will be leaving soon because Chip
and his wife are separating. It breaks my heart.

Rosalynn

I don't mean this to sound like one-upsmanship, but we have 12
grandchildren — each one special in his/her own way. None of them has
lived at the White House with us, but they visit quite often. Family is
very important to both George and me. Even George's political stand
against abortion is personal. We have a granddaughter who was adopted.
George often says that we wouldn't have her if her birth mother would have
chosen abortion.

Barbara

January 24, 1956

We were recently presented with our fourth grandchild. We now have David, Anne, Susan and little Mary Jean. They are all so precious to me. I try to have them stay with us as often as possible. We made over the third floor for them: a playroom, bedrooms and a dining area.

Ike uses this area for his poker stag parties from time to time, and he has his easel set up there, so it can get pretty crowded.

I also bought three birds for their rooms (a canary and two parakeets that we named Gabby, High Glory and Pete). They are lively and sound so pretty. Ike makes me move them from the room when he's playing poker – he says they're too noisy! Gabby is quite the chatterbox – thus the name.

We also have bicycles and even a little electric car for the children to play with. Whenever the tours are over, the children ride up and down the halls of the first floor squealing with delight. These children (and I suppose anyone's children) fill that big White House with joy.

On the other hand, we have Barbara and the children stay here for their safety as well. We received so many threats during Mr. McCarthy's hearings, and we fear what the Communists might do, that Ike had to double the Secret Service detail. While our son John was in Korea, we wanted to have Barbara and the children close by – and protected.

Mamie

I remember that General Eisenhower announced his intention to run for re-election just about the same time that Jack's book "Profiles in Courage" was published. I remember because Jack had just recovered from his spinal surgery and several people had asked him if he were interested in running for Vice President with Adlai Stevenson against Ike. Even though Jack didn't get the nomination, I knew he had his eyes on a bigger role.

Jackie

Jimmy's decided to run for a second term, but he is deep in negotiations for release of the hostages in Iran. He is so busy that I am doing most of the campaigning for him, and I'm exhausted. That damn Khomeini is causing Americans to become disillusioned with Jimmy.

Rosalynn

January 25, 1956

On the 13th, Ike had another "stag" dinner at the White House. This one was highly unusual because the guest list was a secret. Only Ike knew who had been invited. In order to maintain the secrecy, Ike put the place cards on the table himself.

The pow-wow is to decide if Ike should run for another term. I know that Milton and John don't want him to run because of his health. I wasn't sure I wanted him to either, but there are a lot reasons for him to run. I just can't stand the thought that everything he worked for in the first three years of his presidency might go for naught if another Republican came in and changed things – or worse yet, a Democrat!

I was never made privy to who came to the dinner, nor what was decided. I imagine Ike will tell me in his own good time. One thing I've learned is that Ike makes up his own mind, and that's that.

Mamie

I was concerned about Lyndon's health, too, but I wasn't consulted — I was told he was running for a full term, by Lyndon himself.

Lady Bird

After Ronnie was shot, I seriously considered whether or not he should run again. Was it worth it?

Nancy

March 8, 1956

I guess Ike has decided to run for another term. I say, "I guess" because he didn't discuss it with me. I heard it from his secretary, Ann Whitman.

I remember reading in Eleanor's diary that she didn't want FDR to run for a fourth term because of his health, which is exactly how I feel about Ike. I'm constantly worried about the stress of this job on his heart.

I told him at breakfast this morning that I was going to take him to Gettysburg at the end of this term. Period. But he said, "Now Mamie, you know a guy like me can't retire. I need to stay busy doing things – important things. At least for a little while longer. Give me another four years here, and we'll retire to the farm. I promise, we have many years left to enjoy each other."

I hope it's a promise he can keep.

Mamie

David was evidently quite gregarious and very comfortable being in the spotlight. When we were doing the remodeling of the White House, the staff found more than a dozen little notes under the rugs and behind pictures that David had written. They all said: "I will return."

Jackie

David showed me a picture of this birthday party. It looked like a lot of fun. Roy has his arm around Mamie and the rest of the group includes David and his parents John and Barbara, Ike, Mamie's mother Min, and Dale Evans. They are all watching as David blows out the candles. What a joyful photograph it is.

Pat N.

April 4, 1956

I spoil my grandchildren, but I love it. I try to have birthday parties for the grandchildren that are built around something the child likes. Last week was David's 8th birthday. He loves playing cowboys, so we had a group of his friends in to the White House to see a Roy Rogers western. When the children came out of the theater, there was Roy and Dale Evans in person. The children were so surprised! Little David was just beaming.

We had a birthday cake with little plastic horses and a corral. At the end of the party we all sang "Happy Trails to You." The party was a complete success.

I've done the same type of thing for all of my grandchildren. I just love to throw parties!

Mamie

Funny, I don't even remember signing the release for the doctors to operate on Ronnie. I'm sure I did, but I don't remember. There was so much chaos in that hospital. Three of the men who were shot at the same time were being treated there, including Jim Brady. Secret Service people were running in and out, the police were trying to get the area cleared of people who didn't belong there, the press was outside shouting questions at anybody who walked by, phones were ringing off the hook, emergency lights were flashing on the patrol cars and every once in a while a siren could be heard. But I was in a daze.

Nancy

June 9, 1956

Ike was rushed to the hospital again on the 6th. It scared all of us to death. Turns out it was an ileitis attack. The doctors talked all night trying to decide whether to operate or not. One of the doctors didn't think it was necessary, and I agreed with him.

Finally, just after midnight, Dr. Walter Tkach said that if he didn't operate he would lose the patient. They gave me a permission paper to sign, but I just couldn't do it. If something bad happened, I just wouldn't be able to forgive myself.

After more discussions, our son John signed the papers. And, thankfully, Ike made it through the operation just fine and is quite recovered already.

Mamie

Jack and I spent our wedding night at the Waldorf-Astoria and then flew to Mexico City and on to Acapulco. We stayed in a beautiful villa that was on the side of a steep hill overlooking the ocean. It was the home of the President of Mexico. After two relaxing weeks, we went on to San Francisco. While we were in Acapulco and even more so in San Francisco, Jack would go off and leave me for long periods of time. It infuriated me, but it is a pattern of behavior he's continued and I've learned to put up with.

Jackie

We didn't really have a honeymoon. After our wedding we moved to Norfolk. Jimmy was in the Navy and was at sea from Monday until Friday. I was left alone in a strange city, but it made me learn to become independent.
(P.S. Do you suppose Jackie really didn't know what was going on?)

Rosalynn

Jackie was either naïve or blind as to what Jack was up to. It was pretty obvious to me and my circle of friends. As a matter of fact, Jack's escapades made for very interesting cocktail talk.

Nancy

After our wedding in Rye, NY, George and I went to New York City for one night. We saw "Meet Me in St. Louis" at Radio City Music Hall. The next day we took the train to the Cloisters in Sea Island, Georgia. The place was lovely and we promised ourselves we would come back often. However, we didn't get back there until this year. (46 years later!)

Barbara

Bill and I were not planning to take a honeymoon because he was campaigning for Arkansas state attorney general. When my mother found out we weren't going anywhere, she booked a tour to Acapulco. It wasn't all that romantic, though, because she got tickets for my whole family to go with us. Bill hated to sit on the beach relaxing, so he spent the entire honeymoon writing thank you notes to his friends and political acquaintances who came to the wedding. Just another form of campaigning.

HRC

July 1, 1956

Today is our 40th wedding anniversary. It hardly seems possible it's been that long. As an Army wife I spent more than 36 of those years following Ike all over the world.

I remember our honeymoon like it was yesterday. We got away by ourselves for a couple of days. Toward the end of the honeymoon we visited Ike's parents in Kansas. One night Ike went to play poker with some of his childhood buddies and didn't get home by dinnertime. So I called the house where he was playing and told him it was time to come for dinner. He said that he was losing and couldn't quit until he got ahead. I told him that he should come now or not at all. I was sure that would get him to come home, but his mother told me not to be surprised if he didn't show up – and he didn't. He didn't come home until about 2:00 in the morning. I was furious, and we had quite a spat. There have been lots of times over the years that Ike broke my heart, but I wouldn't have stood it for a minute if I didn't respect him so much.

I also remember he had to go away on some military assignment about a month after we got married. I was so upset that I cried and cried. Ike said to me that his country would always come first, and that I

It was hard to be separated as a newlywed. After I had our first child, all that changed. I loved that little boy so much it hurt. He was the center of my life while Jimmy was away. I can't imagine how hard it must be to lose a child.

Rosalynn

would come second. I learned to accept that, but it took a number of years.

The most difficult challenge for our marriage was the death of our three-year-old son Icky. We grew estranged for over a year. Ike kept busy with his work, and I just couldn't seem to get hold of myself. I was miserable. We were living in Panama, the heat was suffocating and I was sick all the time.

Finally, my friend Virginia Conner told me that if I didn't snap out of it I would lose Ike, too. She told me I should "vamp" Ike. Well, I'm no Theda Bara, but I did start dressing better and had my hair done. I had bangs cut and Ike loved my new look. Things got better, and we survived.

Today Ike gave me a ruby heart with this engraving: "I love you better today than the day I met you." I feel the same way.

                                    Mamie

Jack loves to play golf, but he tries to keep that fact quiet. During his campaign, he was playing golf in California. On one hole he hit a shot that looked like it was going to be a hole-in-one, but it landed a few inches from the cup. Jack was relieved. If that ball had gone into the hole, he told me, the word would have gotten out that another golfer was trying to get into the White House.

Jackie

Dick played a few times with Ike. One of the first times they played, they lost. Ike got mad at Dick and told him he was young and should be able to play a lot better. So Dick took lessons, and the next time they played Dick beat him. Ike was furious. Sometimes there was no pleasing him.

Pat

This fall, Ronnie was playing golf at Augusta National when they were told that a terrorist had taken over the pro shop and was holding some hostages. He demanded to speak to the President. Needless to say the Secret Service got Ronnie to the car and out of the area. Ronnie tried to call the guy from the safety of the limousine, but couldn't reach him. The guy finally let the hostages go and was taken into custody a couple of hours later. It was frightening.

Nancy

I finally got back to playing golf after not playing for about 20 years. I wanted to be able to play with George when we retire. So, not long ago we played our first round together. I didn't do very well, but George had the nerve to tell reporters that my game "stunk." Well, I will never play with him again.

Barbara

As a surprise for Bill's 49th birthday this year, I arranged for Johnny Miller to play a round with him at the Jackson Hole Golf Club while we were on vacation. Bill loved it, but the score didn't reflect it. Bill shot an 89 and Johnny shot 69. Oh, well, they had fun.

HRC

August 12, 1956

Golf, golf, golf. Sometimes I think that's the only thing on Ike's mind. He plays at least twice a week when we are in Washington, and twice a day when we go on vacation to Augusta National. Our favorite place to go is Augusta National. It is so pretty. I like the sound of a golf club better than a hunting or fishing lodge. They even have a cottage for us there that is named Mamie's Cabin. Isn't that nice?

Ike practices on the South Lawn of the White House. He hits balls out to the fence. Sometimes they go out into the street and cause quite a traffic jam.

He fancies himself something of a golfer. He has played with real professionals like Sam Snead, Ben Hogan, Byron Nelson, and Arnold Palmer, and I guess he does alright. Once Sam Snead gave Ike a tip. He told Ike to stick his rear end out. The Secret Service man got mad and was going to say something, but Ike just said, "I thought it was out."

Ike's favorite player (at least his closest golfing friend) is Bobby Jones. After Bobby became crippled, he gave Ike his personal golf clubs, since he would not be needing them any more. Ike was so proud to use those clubs. To pay back the favor, Ike painted a portrait of Bobby and gave it to him. It was one of Ike's best paintings, I thought.

One time Ike teamed up with Bob Hope for a round. Mr. Hope kept telling jokes the entire time. It rattled Ike so much that they lost. Ike didn't like having to pay up his $4 bet.

Mamie

That was quite an election. General Eisenhower won by more than ten million votes. I'm glad Jack didn't get the Vice Presidential nomination after all.

Jackie

Lyndon nominated Jack at that convention. He said, "Texas proudly casts its vote for the fighting sailor who wears the scars of battle." I actually think Jack was lucky not to get nominated, not because Eisenhower won, but because his concession speech was eloquent. The Democrats, and the country for that matter, were charmed by him. It got him known so that the 1960 campaign was easier. Lyndon liked Jack very much, and was honored to have been chosen as his Vice President.

Lady Bird

There was a serious "dump Nixon movement" during the Republican convention that year led by Harold Stassen. Of course, it wasn't the first time the party tried to get rid of Dick. Well, he showed the party that Republican voters wanted him. In the New Hampshire and Oregon primaries, 52,000 people wrote Dick's name in under Ike's. The party knew they had to keep him, and I think they're glad they did.

Pat

November 6, 1956

It is election day. We thought this would be an easy election (and it looks like Ike will win), but with everything that's been going on in Egypt and with the Suez Canal I wasn't sure what might happen.

The Suez Canal crisis began last summer. John Foster Dulles cancelled a $56 million loan the United States had promised Egypt to build a dam on the Nile River. I don't know all of the details, except what I read in the papers. The leader of the Egyptian military, Mr. Nasser, got mad, seized the Suez Canal and blocked shipments.

This was very bad for England and France because their petroleum is shipped through the Canal. Then the Premier of Israel ordered his troops to attack Egypt. There had been a festering feud between them for a long time, and I guess this looked like a good excuse. Then England started bombing airfields in Egypt.

Today, we hear that French troops have seized the east side of the Suez Canal. It is all very distressing. We do not want another world war. Here we are about to spend the next four years in the White House. I don't know if I can stand it if we go to war again. I just don't know.

Ike says that the only way to win World War III is to prevent it. I sure hope that's possible.

Mamie

Mamie's right, people were riveted by Joe McCarthy's hearings. They sat for hours in front of the TV or the radio. We called it the "Red Scare." People were convinced that there were communists everywhere in our country. I didn't pay much attention to it, though, because I was busy with my babies.

Barbara

May 2, 1957

Joe McCarthy died today from the effects of drink – and with him one of the darkest eras in American history. All during his hearings he sat with a glass of water in front of him, which he drank constantly. Well, I want you to know that it wasn't water – it was gin.

A lot of people believed what the Senator had to say. We became a nation of paranoids constantly looking at people with suspicion. "Is he a communist?" was the first thought people had when a stranger was around.

But once the witch-hunt was over, once people saw for themselves that we had nothing to fear but fear itself, as the saying goes, I think most Americans were embarrassed by their behavior.

Mamie

We travel by helicopter all the time now. The military and Secret Service decided that the helicopter was safe and thus a better way to travel up here rather than by car. Less chance for some crazy person with a gun to be successful.

Lady Bird

Shortly after Jack took office, I asked Mr. West to show me the bomb shelter at the White House. When we got there I was surprised to see dozens of men who were members of the Signal Corps working there. They used the bomb shelter for a command post and had an elaborate communications system set up. I had planned to use it for a playroom for the children!

Jackie

July 12, 1957

What a thrilling journey we had to Camp David today. We traveled by helicopter! It was my first ride in one. I was amazed that it took only 30 minutes to get here from the White House (instead of the usual 2 hours by car).

I will never forget the ride! My heart was in my throat the whole way. It's so much different than riding in an airplane. In a helicopter you see everything – where you're going, where you've been, where you are! Oh, my, it was exciting.

I'm afraid I may have inflicted permanent marks on Ike's arm where I was holding on for dear life. We landed on the grass near the entrance and the dust and leaves flew every which-a-way. Once on the ground, I realized that I quite enjoyed the ride. They tell me the helicopter is meant for emergency use only, which is a shame as it is such a fast and easy way to travel.

The reason for our trip this time was more of a military exercise than pleasure. The Navy has built a bomb shelter at Camp David (we already have one at the White House that the Trumans built), and we were supposed to inspect it today. In a way it's sad to have to have this shelter, but everyone is afraid of what the Russians might do.

The shelter is quite interesting. There is room for about 200 people. How do you suppose they are going to decide who gets to go in?

My understanding is that there is a written protocol about who goes into the shelter. I haven't seen the list and don't really want to — my name might not be on it!

Betty F.

When we moved the pool and had to reinforce the bomb shelter, I went inside it for a look. I found the diary Mamie left. Evidently, both Jackie and Lady Bird found it, too, because they each wrote little notes in it. So, I did, too.

Pat N.

The bomb shelter diary has become like a guest book. Everybody except Nancy has signed it. But I don't suppose she'd go into a bomb shelter unless absolutely necessary.

HRC

and who has to stay out? And who do you suppose will make that decision?

  You'd never know there was a bomb shelter out here. It's built right out of the rocks underground, and runs underneath the cabins. It's really not noticeable at all. But I was shocked to find out it cost $10 million.

       Mamie

P.S. I left a blank diary in the shelter...just in case.

Yes, Jack and Grace had a wonderful friendship. He admired her and the feeling was mutual. Jack often called her to talk about life in the White House.

Jackie

I remember reading the note that Grace wrote to Eleanor Roosevelt in her diary. She seemed so positive and encouraging of this diary project. So, I am dedicating my diary to Grace Coolidge.

Barbara

July 13, 1957

　　Grace Coolidge died on the 8ᵗʰ. She was quite a woman. As First Lady, Grace did whatever she could to help crippled children and opened the nation's eyes to the needs of the disabled. She was a trained teacher for the deaf prior to becoming First Lady, and often invited students from Clarke School for the Deaf to tour the White House. One of her most beloved guests was Helen Keller.

　　Senator Kennedy gave a wonderful eulogy for Grace. (He's quite an eloquent speaker.) He and Grace were close friends, as I understand it. He said that she was gracious, charming and modest – an ideal First Lady of the Land.

Mamie

Martin Luther King led a group of Negroes to Washington on the 28th. There were over 200,000 people. They marched and sang and gave speeches about the discrimination against them. Mr. King delivered an eloquent speech. His refrain was: "I have a dream." I think it will ring in our consciousness for a long time to come.

Jackie

September 25, 1957

We've had some riots between whites and Negroes in Little Rock, Arkansas this month. Nine Negro children are being kept out of Central High School on the orders of Governor Faubus. The white people are threatening worse violence if they are admitted. Things got so bad that the mayor called the White House asking for federal help.

Ike didn't want to use U.S. troops to fight U.S. citizens — what an unthinkable act — but the local police couldn't restore order and he had no choice. He had to call up the National Guard to help restore the peace.

There are horrible comments being made by some of the southern politicians that this is the Civil War all over again. Senator Talmadge says the President of the United States threatens the South and he should be impeached. Alabama's Governor Folsom said he would disband the National Guard in his state before he'd let Ike call them up. The South Carolina governor resigned his Navy Reserve commission so that he couldn't be forced into service of this kind.

Eventually the Army got the children into the school and things are starting to settle down. But what with this and the Montgomery bus boycott last year, I have a feeling this is just the beginning.

Mamie

We had to entertain a Princess not long ago who thought she was going to stay in the White House. I was exhausted and it was just six weeks after Patrick's death, so I asked Mr. West to make the Queen's Room and Lincoln's bedroom look like they weren't available for guests. He is so clever. He had paint cans, ladders, and dirty brushes put in the rooms and draped the furniture. After dinner, Jack walked past the two rooms with the Princess. He told her "This is where you would have spent the night if Jackie hadn't been redecorating again." Voila! No unwanted guest!

Jackie

Prince Charles and Princess Anne stayed with us at Camp David in July. They are about the same age as our girls. They rode bicycles and went swimming. We had a cookout with hamburgers and banana splits for dessert.

Pat N.

There have been five queens who have stayed in the Queen's Room: Queen Elizabeth (the Queen Mother), Queen Wilhelmina and Queen Juliana of the Netherlands, Queen Frederika of Greece and Queen Elizabeth II. It is decorated in rose and white with antique furniture. I think the most interesting item is the toilet - it looks like a wicker chair.

Nancy

October 25, 1957

We had a perfectly wonderful visit from Queen Elizabeth and Prince Philip. They stayed with us in the White House for four days (along with fifteen ladies- and men-in-waiting). After they left, Ike said that if they'd have stayed any longer we'd be calling them Liz and Phil.

The logistics for sleeping were very difficult. The Queen, of course, slept in the Queen's Room. Her husband slept in Lincoln's bedroom. I had to stack the rest of them all over the second and third floors!

We had a beautiful state dinner for them with about a hundred guests, and afterwards we listened to the Fred Waring orchestra. The evening was very formal and carefully planned. The Chief Usher, Mr. West, had the butlers practice serving and clearing so that everything would run smoothly. And it did, almost.

After the meal, Ike got up and gave a toast to the Queen. Then it was her turn. She is so young and soft-spoken that the room went completely silent. Just as she was finishing the toast, one of the butlers dropped a tray. Ordinarily, we never would have noticed with everyone talking, but, wouldn't you know, it happened when everyone was quiet and the Queen of England was speaking.

I was mortified. The next day I made sure the butler was dismissed. I believe you must deal with these domestic decisions swiftly and with certainty.

Mamie

Jack is determined to get ahead of the Russians. He knows that American technology can do it, but the American people have been skeptical. He has promised that the U.S. will put a man on the moon before the end of this decade. Last month, the U.S. launched Alan Shepard into space and brought him back safely. It was remarkable. Everyone is ecstatic.

Jackie

Lyndon was angry at the time because the Air Force had very powerful missiles, but Ike wouldn't let the civilian scientists have them. The Senate felt this slowed down the progress of the space program. Ike eventually reversed his decision and now the civilians and military are working together on putting a man on the moon.

Lady Bird

When I was a kid, we would lie on the ground at night staring up at the sky and watch for satellites. If you looked very carefully, you could see one or two slowly move across the sky. It was hard because of all the stars, but once you spotted one it was so exciting.

HRC

November 10, 1957

The first man-made satellite to orbit the earth was launched by Russia in October. They call it Sputnik. Funny name, don't you think? It means "fellow traveler." Then on November 3rd, Sputnik II went into orbit, this time with a dog named Laika on board. On the radio, we can hear the satellite go beep, beep, beep.

I think it's very exciting scientifically speaking, but no one else in the White House does, so I have to keep quiet about it. They are looking at it in military terms. Everyone thinks that the Russians will soon land on the moon and then, for all intents and purposes, would be the leaders of the world because they have the ability to blow the rest of us up. With the touch of a button in Moscow, Washington would vanish.

Ike is trying to stay calm, but Congress is all whipped into a frenzy. Senate Majority Leader Lyndon Johnson said that the Roman Empire controlled the world because they built the roads. Then the British Empire dominated because they built better boats. Now the Soviets control outer space.

People are saying that instead of being called Project Vanguard, the American space program should be called Project Rearguard. The New York Times swears that one of their reporters called the U.S. Space Agency and was asked by the receptionist, "Are you calling _for_ information or _with_ information."

We were only happy to have helped out at the dinner. We had such short notice I didn't have time to do my hair. It was a mess.

Pat N.

November 26, 1957

Ike suffered a stroke yesterday. The doctors say he will be ok, but I am beside myself with worry. Why did I let him run for a second term? I knew something like this would happen. Since his heart attack two years ago, every time he gets up to make a big speech I live in fear that he will drop dead on the spot.

It happened just a few hours before another state dinner we were giving – this time for the King of Morocco. I wanted to cancel the evening's plans because Dr. Snyder absolutely forbade Ike from attending, but Ike wouldn't hear of it. He insisted the dinner go on with me as the hostess. If I didn't agree to it, he'd get dressed and go himself. My Ike can be mighty stubborn, but sometimes I do get tired of being ordered around.

I went, of course. I called Vice President and Mrs. Nixon and asked them to help me host the dinner. They are such sports. Everything went well, but it seemed so dull and dark in the dining room. When Ike's not with me, there doesn't seem to be any light in the room.

Mamie

November 28, 1957

I can't believe it. Just three days after his stroke, Ike is flying off to Paris for a meeting of the NATO heads of government. He's feeling much better, but so soon after a major health problem? I think he's lost his mind!

Mamie

I wonder what Mamie would think about how far we've come in just 40 years? We've been to the moon several times, built a space station (with the Russians!), and our spaceships land like airplanes instead of plopping down in the ocean. Mamie, we did it!

HRC

December 7, 1957

Yesterday, the first U.S. satellite was supposed to be launched from Cape Canaveral. The pressure to get a satellite in orbit has been tremendous. No one wants the Russians to get any further ahead of us in the space race. The launch was broadcast on TV across the country. Everyone saw the Vanguard take off from Cape Canaveral for a few seconds, then fall back down and crash. The explosion was terrific. No one was hurt, but it caused a lot of grumbling in the press. The headlines this morning called the launch either: Flopnik or Kaputnik.

Poor Ike. He wants to go more slowly with this whole thing, but Congress, the press and even the American people are screaming for us to get a satellite in orbit. Lots of people want the government to put money into the education of more scientists, but Ike doesn't want to do that either. Oh, boy, I wonder how this will end?

Mamie

Lyndon was pursuing me pretty aggressively when we first met (asked me to marry him on our first date), but I was trying to slow things down. He told me he was ambitious and in love with me. But I told him I didn't want him if he was going into politics. Then he gave me the Johnson Treatment (he took my face in his huge hands and just held me tenderly) and I melted.

Lady Bird

Dick asked me to marry him on our first date, too, but I wasn't interested. He kept asking, and I kept saying no. He was so determined that he even drove me on dates with other boys. After eight or nine months of this, I finally said yes. He promised to take me places, and I sure wanted to get out of my small hometown.

Pat N.

Jimmy took me away from my small town, too, and we moved to San Diego, Connecticut and Hawaii. Life was so exciting for me, but about seven years later he left the Navy and we moved back to Plains. I cried and cried.

Rosalynn

George and I were so suited to one another that he didn't even have to propose. We just knew we would get married.

Barbara

July 1, 1958

This is our 42nd wedding anniversary. Quite a milestone. It seems like yesterday that we met. Ike and I met at a lawn party at Fort Sam Houston. It was a beautiful Sunday afternoon in October 1915. I was 18 years old. I remember that one of the men had been talking about this officer named Eisenhower, saying he was a born woman hater, which of course was intriguing. Then all of a sudden, Ike came across the street and joined the party.

He looked so handsome in his uniform – blond, slim and snappy looking. He was Officer of the Day so couldn't stay at the party long. He had to go inspect the guard, which meant walking around the compound. As he left, he asked me to walk with him. I agreed, but regretted it later. He was dressed for the three-mile hike around the post, but I had on brand new lace-up boots that practically crippled me by the end of the tour!

At one point during the walk, Ike told me not to look up. We were passing a barracks and the men were changing clothes. I guess they didn't pull down the shades (not expecting any women to be walking around, of course!). Well, naturally, when he told me not to look, I immediately did. It was a natural reaction. Ike laughed and laughed, and said wasn't that just like a woman. We were married less than a year later.

Mamie

I know that Jack has not been faithful to me during our marriage. On his inauguration night, without saying anything, he left for a while. When he came back he was carrying a copy of the "Washington Post." He wanted me to think he'd gone out to buy a copy of the newspaper. Later I found out from friends that he'd gone to a party with Frank Sinatra, and spent time with Angie Dickinson. But good comes with bad, and sometimes the heartbreak is worth the pain - especially now. I am meeting royalty and heads of state, I travel to exotic spots, I am experiencing things I never would have if I weren't married to Jack.

Jackie

It's a shame that Eleanor let Lucy Rutherford come between her and FDR. Lucy was nothing more than a fly on the wedding cake. I learned early in our marriage that Lyndon equated sex with power. I didn't think much about it – my father had several lady friends in addition to his wife. I guess I just thought that's the way things were.

Lady Bird

When Bill was running for governor, I hired a private detective to follow him. He gave me a list of eight women Bill was seeing at that time. So his recent indiscretions are not a surprise to me - but that doesn't mean it doesn't hurt.

HRC

July 2, 1958

     I didn't sleep very well last night. I guess with the anniversary on my mind, I somehow got to thinking about Ike and Kay Summersby. I've put off writing about this for a long time, but I guess it needs to be addressed and this is as good a time as any. Mrs. Roosevelt was quite candid in her diary about Lucy Rutherford and FDR. Maybe if I write about it I can finally put it in the past.

     When Ike was in Europe during WWII, there were many rumors about an affair he was having with his beautiful driver. It was hard on me to hear these stories being thousands of miles away from him. I was very lonely, but then I spent most of my married life feeling lonely because of Ike's job.

     There had been other rumors about Ike having close female companions over the years, but this time was different. There were pictures of them in the newspaper. This rumor had a face, a young and beautiful one at that. I wrote to Ike that I was concerned about what was being said, but he said that I was over-reacting. He told me that he loved only me. Of course I truly believed that, but then why didn't he transfer Kay to another unit? I mean, how indispensable could a driver be?

     My biggest fear was that Ike had created a life without me. I guess I was jealous. I wanted to be the woman he needed, but I couldn't be when we were so far apart.

I have made peace with myself over the years about Kay and Ike. Yes, there may have been some intimacy between them, but I don't think about it. After all, he came home to me.

Mamie

We entertained Soviet President Leonid Brezhnev at the White House for two days, and then at Camp David. He and Dick are discussing nuclear weapons control. At the White House it was all business, but once out here everyone relaxed. Dick gave Mr. Brezhnev a brand new Lincoln Continental. He loves cars and test drove it around here - driving much too fast for these narrow, winding roads. I can't imagine what would have happened to our relations with the Soviet Union if he would have driven it off the side of the mountain!

Pat N.

Camp David was purposefully chosen over the White House for the meetings between Anwar Sadat and Menachem Begin. There was a very informal atmosphere that we hoped would encourage open discussions. And we didn't spend all the time in meetings — people played chess, rode bicycles, played tennis and we showed over 55 movies during the summit.

Rosalynn

Prime Minister Margaret Thatcher has been here twice to meet with Ronnie. She enjoys riding around in the golf cart.

Nancy

Soviet President Mikhail Gorbachev was invited to our home in Kennebunkport, but said he'd rather meet at Camp David. He had heard so much about it. He and George played a few games of horseshoes.

Barbara

March 21, 1959

We are out at the camp for a few days while Ike and British Prime Minister Harold Macmillan meet. They are going to talk about how to save Berlin. I guess the Russians are trying to shut it off from the rest of the world. I don't understand these things – and don't really want to, truth be told.

I remember that Mrs. Roosevelt wrote in her diary that Prime Minister Churchill came out here several times for diplomatic meetings with FDR. I can see how different discussions are here compared to discussions at the White House. The White House is very formal and clearly leaves a visiting dignitary at a disadvantage. Camp David is perfect: quiet, soothing, informal, and a long way from TV cameras! (At least FDR didn't have to worry about that.)

After dinner tonight, we are going to watch a movie called "The Big Country" with Charlton Heston and Gregory Peck. It's a Western – Ike's favorite kind of movie. I'm kind of sick of seeing them, though. I think we've watched this one three or four times. I'd like to see my favorite, "Gigi" with that dreamy Maurice Chevalier. Oh well, maybe another time.

It is so cold tonight. The wind seems to come right through the walls. I hope we have enough blankets for everyone.

Mamie

Our daughter Luci had her wedding reception at the White House, and Lynda had both her wedding and reception there. They were beautiful events. Lynda's was the first White House wedding in 53 years. The only close brush with disaster we had was when Lyndon wanted his dog Yuki to be in the family portrait. I put a stop to that immediately.

Lady Bird

Tricia's wedding last month was the first to be held in the Rose Garden. It was quite lovely despite the threat of rain all day. The wedding cake almost collapsed because of the humidity, but we got it cut and served just in time. Both of the Johnson girls came to the wedding as well as Alice Roosevelt Longworth (who was herself a White House bride).

Pat N.

Our daughter Doro got married at Camp David last weekend (the first wedding at the Camp). The ceremony was in the chapel and there was an outdoor reception. The wedding was "informal," so George thought that meant he could wear golf clothes. He didn't even have a tie, so we had to scramble to find one. A funny moment happened when the couple knelt at the altar. Those of us in the congregation noticed that someone had stuck Bush re-election campaign stickers on the bottom of the groom's shoes!

Barbara

July 4, 1959

Ike and I are out here at Camp David for a few days on our "honeymoon." I like saying that, sure gives some people a start. Actually, we repeated our wedding vows at the White House a few days ago. It was so romantic. The ceremony was in the East Room, and all our friends were there, plus John, Barbara and the grandchildren.

I was so nervous. That seems kind of silly after 43 years of marriage, but I was. I wore a lovely strapless, soft pink gown with a full tulle skirt. I had an elbow-length veil and carried a huge white and pink bouquet of lilies-of-the-valley, roses and carnations. Ike was handsome, as always, in his white dinner jacket.

We had a grand dinner to celebrate. Ike and I even got to dance to "The Anniversary Waltz." It was a fun evening and everyone seemed to enjoy themselves.

Mamie

Protocol in the White House is pretty controlled nowadays. At one dinner, however, the White House Social Aide almost got into a fight with Muhammed Ali. All the guests had been seated except Ali and his wife. Protocol is that everyone has to be in the room before the President comes in (and we were waiting to enter). The Aide found the couple lollygagging in the hall looking at the artwork. He asked them to hurry, but Ali wanted to know who was going to make him. The Aide (in a teasing manner) put up his dukes and said he was. Ali lifted his huge fists and struck a serious fighting pose that almost made the Aide pass out from fear. Fortunately Ali's wife told her husband to quit fooling around and get to dinner.

Rosalynn

We held a dinner once for just-released Prisoners of War and their spouses - about 1500 people. In order for everyone to be in the same room, we had to have a tent put up on the White House South Lawn. Unfortunately, it rained very hard the day before and continued the day of the dinner. Table legs and chairs were sinking into the soft ground. It was a mess. Anyway, as protocol demands, the guests were to stand when the President and I entered and remain standing until we were seated at our table - at the far end of the tent. As we walked across the huge tent, Dick and I could see that the women (in their high heels) were slowly getting shorter as they stood there sinking into the wet grass. But no one moved or sat down. It was one of the funniest things I've ever seen - like a Monty Python skit!

Pat N.

My first indication of the formality at the White House happened shortly after we moved in. I picked up one of the White House phones and asked to speak to Jimmy. The Operator said, "Jimmy who?" (Even the family has to refer to him as the President when speaking to staff.)

Rosalynn

September 16, 1959

Last night, we had the first of several state dinners planned for the season. Nikita Khrushchev and his wife were here. I spent weeks trying to decide what to serve. I finally settled on a traditional American meal: turkey, dressing, cranberry sauce, sweet potatoes and all the rest.

Things with the Russians are very uneasy right now, and I wanted everything to be just right. I planned a formal evening, but Mr. Khrushchev insisted on wearing a plain old business suit. His wife wore a street length dress. Well, I wasn't going to let them dictate protocol. I wore a gold brocade ball gown and Ike was in white tie.

The evening didn't get off to a good start. Ike is always very punctual, but I'm not. Since I was so nervous about the dinner, it took me longer to get dressed. Ike was furious. When I finally was ready, he said, "Do you realize you've kept the President of the United States waiting?" I said, "Why no. I've been busy making myself pretty for my husband."

Mamie

When Eleanor Roosevelt entertained the King and Queen of England, she invited them to her cottage at Val-Kill. She served hot dogs and all the trimmings, much to the horror of her mother-in-law. King George wanted to know what the "delicacy" was and Eleanor said hot dogs - they were the only thing she knew how to cook besides scrambled eggs.

HRC

September 26, 1959

  Prime Minister Khrushchev and Ike are meeting again
- this time out here at Camp David. Mr. K. has just
returned from visiting New York, California and Iowa. He's
been making quite a spectacle of himself across the country.

  I don't know how much they are getting accomplished.
I hear raised voices from time to time. They are out on the
sun porch so their voices carry all over. They agree on at
least one thing: we found out that Mr. K. loves Westerns.
He told us that he and Josef Stalin used to watch them
together all the time. I guess tonight we'll get to see "High
Noon," or "Shane," or if we're real lucky "The Big County"
for the one hundredth time.

  For lunch today, to continue our American dining fare,
we are going to have frankfurters and baked beans. Later,
Ike is going to take Mr. K. to Gettysburg to show him our
farmhouse. I don't know if I like the thought of them going
to our home. It's one thing to host a political adversary at
the White House or Camp David, but to take him to our
private home seems wrong to me. Ike tells me that he wants
Mr. Khrushchev to see how a typical American family lives
- our grandchildren will be there.

  Of course I don't say anything. It's up to the men to
take care of these things.

Mamie

The dances kids do today are crazy! Luci loves to dance the Dog, the Monkey, the Chicken, the Watusi and the Frug. The names alone are crazy — I don't even know what a Frug is. The Fox Trot is more my taste.

Lady Bird

I'm not "with" the new clothing styles. Mini skirts are 10 inches above the knees or more. Both my girls wear them, but I wouldn't dream of it. One look at my legs and the fashion designers would put everyone in floor-length dresses again.

Pat N.

I can't quite get excited about aerobics, the new way to exercise. I love to dance, but aerobics is too much like work.

Betty F.

For me, it's Punk rock. I don't understand what the attraction is. It actually looks dangerous!

Barbara

October 10, 1959

I think Ike and I are getting old. My niece was here recently, and it was quite clear to me that I haven't been keeping up on what's going on in this modern world.

She was telling us about Beatniks. They are (to quote her) "groovy guys that recite poetry and are with it." With what? I wanted to know, but she just rolled her eyes. Well, I like poetry the same as the next person, but I guess I just don't understand why they have to walk around snapping their fingers and saying "cool man" and "groovy" all the time.

I used to love to dance, but I just don't seem to appreciate the new rock and roll music. Elvis Presley just makes noise as far as I'm concerned. I much prefer the old standards played by bands like Lawrence Welk.

And Ike hates the new abstract art. He fancies himself something of an artist (amateur though he is), and he just can't bring himself to understand this new type of art. I don't mind it so much, though. I think it's kind of fun.

I see so many youngsters playing with a new toy called the Hula-hoop. I wouldn't dare try one; I'd probably break something. Besides, it looks like a lot of work to me.

We just seem out of touch. So, I guess we _are_ getting old.

Mamie

I went on a goodwill tour of India and Pakistan, too, however I went without Jack. My sister was with me, but I was scared to death. I was afraid I might say something wrong. The trip turned out just fine, though. Indira Gandhi was so gracious – all of the Indian people were. They gave me many gifts (including an elephant and two tiger cubs that we sent to a zoo.). But I was so glad to get home. I missed my family, and I was exhausted.

Jackie

The only goodwill trip I took alone was to head the U.S. delegation at the inauguration of the president of Costa Rica. President and Mrs. Calderon were the most gracious people you'd ever want to meet. When the U.S. delegation walked into the stadium for the ceremony, we received a standing ovation. It was quite moving.

Barbara

December 23, 1959

Ike is finally home after a nine-day "goodwill tour" of eleven countries. Honestly, after all he's been through with his health, I was just beside myself that he decided to do this - it's 22,000 miles for crying out loud. He is planning three of these goodwill trips before his term is over next year.

He went to Iran, India, Pakistan, Afghanistan and other countries that are struggling to survive. He wanted to bring a message of hope and encouragement, and ensure them that the United States was a friend.

Well, it was too much for me, and I wasn't afraid to admit it. Barbara and John went along with Ike. Barbara acted as my representative. The cables I received indicated she did a fine job, and she seemed to enjoy it.

Everyone arrived home in good shape. I must say that the reports in the newspapers are calling the goodwill tour a complete success. Queen Elizabeth sent Ike a letter saying she admired his journey to so many countries. She said she would never again be able to complain that she had too much to do when she travels in the future.

Mamie

Francis Gary Powers is now home safely. The U.S. worked out an exchange: Mr. Powers for a Russian spy who had been convicted in America. I know that General Eisenhower was disappointed that he couldn't get Mr. Powers released during his administration. Jack was relieved when it was all over.

Jackie

Nothing makes a President feel more helpless than when Americans are held as hostages. The student militants who took over the U.S. Embassy in Teheran have been holding 52 American hostages for more than a year now. Jimmy has desperately tried to win their release, even trying a military rescue attempt. Even though he lost the election last month (oddly enough election day was one year to the day of the embassy takeover), he is working like mad to get this resolved. He would like nothing more than to have them released before he leaves office.

Rosalynn

People say that the timing of the hostage release on Ronnie's inauguration day was planned as a theatrical event. I don't think that's true, but so what if it was? At least they are home.

Nancy

May 5, 1960

We have received word that Gary Powers, a pilot, has been shot down and captured by the Russians. He was flying a U-2 plane on a spying mission. These missions have been going on for some time; the first flight was in 1956. Supposedly, the last spy mission was to have taken place on April 9th, but Allen Dulles, who's the head of the CIA, insisted on one more flight.

Our son John thinks Dulles ought to be fired, but Ike said he wasn't going to let an underling take the blame. In his best military style, Ike as Commander-in-Chief was taking full responsibility (even though he is furious at Allen).

In his press conference today, Ike said that the reason the U.S. was sending out spy planes was to avoid another surprise attack like what happened at Pearl Harbor. I think Americans will understand and accept that.

We just pray for the safe return of Mr. Powers.

Mamie

Dick had no intention of asking for Ike's help. He wanted to win on his own. Dick was bitterly disappointed when he didn't win that election, but he's here now. I hope he's happy.

Pat N.

June 12, 1960

Ike is off again on his third (and last, thank goodness) goodwill tour. He is going to Alaska, Manila, Seoul, and Hawaii among other stops.

His stops in Alaska and Hawaii are to welcome them as our two newest states. Imagine that. I never thought I'd live to see two new states added to our union. Mostly, I guess, they were added because of their strategic locations. Not to mention the fact that we've had military bases in both places for a long time.

Barbara and John are going with Ike again. I just can't manage all that traveling. My legs would swell up like balloons. So, I'll just stay here and mind the store.

I continue to be worried about Ike's health. As a matter of fact, I let it be known to the people who are running Dick Nixon's campaign that they shouldn't ask Ike to help. He just shouldn't be running all over making speeches and so forth. They assure me that they won't ask.

Mamie

Mr. West and the staff are wonderful. Lyndon likes to stay up late and work. When he finishes he sometimes likes to have a late dinner. The butlers were having to stay after midnight sometimes, so I asked Mr. West if they couldn't have something prepared that I could warm up whenever Lyndon wanted. That way we could send the butlers home at eight o'clock like they are supposed to. Well, the butlers were quite indignant. They said that they had served Presidents and First Ladies every meal formally for almost 200 years, even if it's a cheese sandwich or a bowl of chili. They would never let the President of the United States serve himself.

Lady Bird

November 27, 1960

We hosted our last gala on the 25th. It was meant to be a celebration of Dick Nixon's election as president, but someone else won. Senator Kennedy is our new president.

Anyway, I didn't want to let the arrangements go for naught, so I decided to hold a Coming Out party for my two nieces, Ellen and Mamie Moore.

Everything was perfect. We had about 500 guests for tea. It was so pretty, there were flowers everywhere. The White House staff is so flexible. I don't know how they do it. Mr. West and his staff are magicians. They can turn things on a dime and leave you nine cents change. First we were going to hold an evening dinner celebration for important Washington politicians, and then we end up holding an afternoon tea for two young women. You never would have known it was planned any other way.

Mamie

Sometimes Jerry gets a little exuberant and steps on his own toes. He says things he doesn't mean. Ready, fire, aim — as they say. I try to be there to help if I can.

Betty F.

I admire the "eyes and ears" role that Eleanor Roosevelt played for FDR and have tried to do the same for Jimmy. We were partners on the farm, and we are partners in the White House. I try to protect him.

Rosalynn

After Ronnie was shot, I was very careful to watch how he acted and what he said. Sometimes his memory gives him a little trouble now, so I keep pretty close tabs on him.

Nancy

January 10, 1961

Ike is preparing his farewell address to the nation. It will be delivered on the 17th. I have no idea what he will talk about, but I know he is very concerned about it - not from a delivery point (we have Robert Montgomery to thank for that), but from a deeper, psychological point.

Ever since his stoke in November of 1957 he's been worried about televised speeches. He has all of his mental faculties, but he's afraid he might accidentally say something he shouldn't. Before the stroke, he was able to control what he said, be vague when he needed to be. But since the stroke, he's worried he might blurt out a secret or make a mistake. It could be quite dangerous. Especially now that he has the briefcase that has all the codes to set off a nuclear bomb. The men call it the "football." I think that sounds too much like a game rather than the horrific weapon it is. It scares me to death. I know why Ike is afraid of saying something wrong.

I have been keeping a pretty close eye on him from a health standpoint for the past six years, but it never occurred to me that I should watch what he says, too. He never said anything to me about it before. That's why I was so surprised when he confided in me today.

As First Ladies, I guess we have a duty to our husbands and the country to closely monitor his activities. We should not try to change or control what he does, but pay attention to any little differences in what he says or how he acts. Ike and I have been married so long that we

George and I have been together a long time, too. We're like a pair of old slippers: a little worn, a little threadbare, but comfortable.

                                                          Barbara

breath in unison sometimes. Only we First Ladies know our husbands well enough to pick up on any peculiarities. I wish I had figured this out earlier, but at least I can pass along the hint to the rest of you.

Being First Lady is a lot more complicated than I at first thought. I've had a good time these last eight years being a White Housewife and haven't concerned myself much with the goings on in the West Wing. But I think you future First Ladies will have to become more involved. You will need to stay on your toes. You can do it!

Mamie

January 11, 1961

Well, Ike has finally completed his service to the American people. I came out to Camp David one more time to put the diary away and to pack up a few things. (I have got to remember to take Ike's golf clubs. He must have told me not to forget them a hundred times!)

Imagine. More than two-thirds of our lives have been spent in the military and in public service. I'm looking forward to just being on our own, but I will miss this life.

I'll let you in on a little secret: I have a canvas chair at Gettysburg – you know like a movie director's. On the back of it I stenciled: First Lady. Just to make sure nobody forgets!

The presidential campaign was very interesting this year. Since Ike wasn't running for office, I could be a spectator. I'm amazed at how important television has become in this election. I guess TV is no longer just for entertainment.

We've been used to getting all of our information from the newspapers, where men were judged on the facts. Now we have this new medium that puts greater emphasis on personalities.

It amazes me how credible the public perceives you to be if you are attractive and can handle the glare of TV lights. Jack and Jackie Kennedy are young, handsome, poised people, while Dick is, well, more plain.

Mamie and Ike enjoyed eight years of blissful retirement before he died. After that, Mamie stayed on at Gettysburg until last week when she, too, passed on. Happy trails to you, Mamie.

Rosalynn

I believed this, too, but after the Health Care fiasco I've become pretty gun-shy. I read some of the things that are said about me and how things I say get twisted around, and I think ugh, I wouldn't like her either.

HRC

We have had handsome first families before and plain ones. But we weren't concerned about that. We were more interested in _what_ was said, not _how_ it was said.

Maybe it's naive of me, but I think that future First Ladies will have a much more public role to play. She will be more involved in the campaigns. I think she will have to have a deep understanding of her husband's policies and be prepared to defend them. And, I think she will be completely linked to the presidency. How well she does in the public eye will help determine how people feel about the president. And vice versa, I suppose.

It's time for me to leave my job and hand over the pen, as it were, to our new First Lady. I will leave this diary, plus Mrs. Roosevelt's and Mrs. Truman's in the armoire along with a brand new one for Mrs. Kennedy. These diaries are the beginning of a very nice tradition.

We will drive over to Gettysburg after the inauguration. It will seem strange to be on our own again, no staff under foot, no politicians looking for something, no Secret Service hovering around. Hmmm. Now that sounds kind of nice.

My very best to you all.

Devotedly,
Mamie Doud Eisenhower

BIOGRAPHY

Mamie Geneva Doud Eisenhower

Mamie Eisenhower's bangs and sparkling blue eyes were as much trademarks of an administration as the President's famous grin. Her outgoing manner, her feminine love of pretty clothes and jewelry, and her obvious pride in husband and home made her a very popular First Lady.

Born in Boone, Iowa, Mamie Geneva Doud moved with her family to Colorado when she was seven. Her father retired from business, and Mamie and her three sisters grew up in a large house in Denver. During winters the family made long visits to relatives in the milder climate of San Antonio, Texas.

There, in 1915, at Fort Sam Houston, Mamie met Dwight D. Eisenhower, a young second lieutenant on his first tour of duty. She drew his attention instantly, he recalled: "a vivacious and attractive girl, smaller than average, saucy in the look about her face and in her whole attitude." On St. Valentine's Day in 1916 he gave her a miniature of his West Point class ring to seal a formal engagement; they were married at the Doud home in Denver on July 1.

For years Mamie Eisenhower's life followed the pattern of other Army wives: a succession of posts in the United States, in the Panama Canal Zone; duty in France, in the Philippines. She once estimated that in 37 years she had unpacked her household at least 27 times. Each move meant another step in the career ladder for her husband, with increasing responsibilities for her.

The first son Doud Dwight or "Icky," who was born in 1917, died of scarlet fever in 1921. A second child, John, was born in 1922 in Denver. Like his father he had a career in the army; later he became an author and served as ambassador to Belgium.

During World War II, while promotion and fame came to "Ike," his wife lived in Washington. After he became president of Columbia University in 1948, the Eisenhowers purchased a farm at Gettysburg, Pennsylvania. It was the first home they had ever owned. His duties as commander of North Atlantic Treaty Organization forces—and hers as his hostess at a chateau near Paris—delayed work on their dream home, finally completed in 1955. They celebrated with a housewarming picnic for the staff from their last temporary quarters: the White House.

When Eisenhower had campaigned for President, his wife cheerfully shared his travels; when he was inaugurated in 1953, the American people warmly welcomed her as First Lady. Diplomacy—and air travel—in the postwar world brought changes in their official hospitality. The Eisenhowers entertained an unprecedented number of heads of state and leaders of foreign governments, and Mamie's evident enjoyment of her role endeared her to her guests and to the public.

In 1961 the Eisenhowers returned to Gettysburg for eight years of contented retirement together. After her husband's death in 1969, Mamie continued to live on the farm, devoting more of her time to her family and friends. Mamie Eisenhower died on November 1, 1979. She is buried beside her husband in a small chapel on the grounds of the Eisenhower Library in Abilene, Kansas.

The First Lady biographies presented here are from the book *The First Ladies* written by Margaret Brown Klapthor and Allida Black (contributing author), published by the White House Historical Association with the cooperation of the National Geographic Society

EXCERPT FROM THE NEXT DIARY

Jackie Kennedy (1961 – 1963)

November 15, 1963

Things are getting back to normal around here after dear little Patrick's death. I am finally feeling almost back to my old self again.

On the 12th, I played hostess to over 2,000 poor children on the White House lawn. We played games and served cocoa and sugar cookies – the cook tells me he made 10,000 cookies.

The Black Watch Regiment from Scotland played bagpipes and marched much to the delight of the children. Even Jack came out of his office for a while to watch. He loved it.

Jack has been so different since Patrick's death. After I got back from Greece, he became very solicitous of me and quite loving. We hold hands whenever we are together. He puts his arm around me and even kisses me in public (something he never did before). I feel like we have turned a corner in our relationship.

Normally I don't like to go on political trips with Jack, but I've decided to go with him to Texas next week. I want him to know how much I appreciate him. He's just going for a few days, and it will be nice to have some time together away from the White House.

I always believed that, given time, Jack would learn to love me.

Jackie

Research Bibliography

Angelo, Bonnie. *First Mothers*. NewYork:
HarperCollins. 2000.

Anthony, Carl Sferrazza. *America's First Families*.
New York: Simon & Schuster. 2000.

Anthony, Carl Sferrazza. *First Ladies. Volume 1*.
New York: William Morrow. 1990.

Anthony, Carl Sferrazza. *First Ladies. Volume 2*.
New York: William Morrow. 1991.

Baldwin, Paul. *The 365 Most Important Events of the
Twentieth Century*. New York: William Morrow. 1999

Bauer, Stephen M. *At Ease In The White House*.
New York: Carol Publishing. 1991.

Berman, Louis A. *Proverb Wit & Wisdom*. New York:
Penquin Putnam. 1997.

Boller, Jr., Paul F. *Presidential Wives*. New York:
Oxford University Press. 1988.

Bush, Barbara. *Barbara BushA Memoir*. New York:
Charles Scribner's Sons. 1994.

Campbell, Shepherd and Peter Landau.
Presidential Lies. Simon & Schuster MacMillan.
1996.

Carpenter, Liz. *Ruffles & Flourishes*. College
Station, TX: Texas A & M University Press. 1993.

Carter, Rosalynn. *First Lady from Plains*. New York:
Houghton Mifflin. 1984.

Cook, Blanche Wiesen. *Eleanor Roosevelt. Volume 2*.
New York: Penguin Putnam. 1999.

Doherty, Robert H. Editor. *The First Ladies
Cookbook*, Chicago: Home Library Press. 1965

Eisenhower, Susan. *Mrs. Ike*. New York: Farrar
Straus Giroux: 1996.

Flexner, Stuart & Doris. *The Pessimist's Guide to
History*. New York: HarperCollins. 2000.

Garrison, Webb. *White House Ladies*. Nashville: Rutledge Hill Press. 1996.

Gergen, David. *Eyewitness to Power*. New York: Simon & Schuster. 2000.

Gilbert, Martin. *A History of the Twentieth Century*. Volume Three. New York: William Morrow. 1999.

Goodwin, Doris Kearns. *No Ordinary Times*. New York: Simon & Schuster. 1994.

Halberstam, David. *The Fifties*. New York: Random House. 1993

Heymann, C. David. *A Woman Named Jackie*. New York: Carol Publishing. 1994.

Johnson, Paul. *A History of The American People*. New York: HarperCollins. 1997.

Joyce, Robert D. *Astonishing Century*. Santa Ana, Ca: Pygmalion Press. 1999

Kelley, Kitty. *Nancy Reagan the Unauthorized Biography*. New York: Simon & Schuster. 1991.

Kessler, Ronald. *Inside The White House*. New York: Simon & Schuster. 1995.

Leaming, Barbara. *Mrs. Kennedy*. New York: The Free Press: 2001

Manchester, William. *The Glory & The Dream* .New York: Little, Brown, 1973.

Margolis, Jon. *The Last Innocent Year*. New York: HarperCollins. 1999.

Martin, Kati. *Hidden Power*. New York: Pantheon Books. 2001

McCullough, David. *Truman*. New York: Simon & Schuster. 1992.

Melich, Tanya. *The Republican War Against Women*. New York: Bantam. 1996.

Milton, Joyce. *The First Partner Hillary Rodham Clinton*. New York: William Morrow. 1999.

Montgomery, Ruth. *Mrs. LBJ*. New York: Holt, Rinehart & Winston. 1964.

Nelson, W. Dale. *The President is at Camp David.* Syracuse: Syracuse University Press. 1995.

Nix, S. Michele. *Women at the Podium.* New York: HarperCollins. 2000

Perret, Geoffrey. *Eisenhower.* Holbrook, MA: Adams Media. 1999.

Pitch, Anthony S. *Exclusively First Ladies Trivia.* Potomac, MD: Mino Publications. 1998.

Reagan, Nancy. *I Love You, Ronnie.* New York: Random House. 2000.

Reagan, Nancy. *My Turn the Memoirs of Nancy Reagan.* New York: Random House. 1989.

Rollo, Vera Foster. *The Presidents and Their Pets.* Lanham, Maryland: Maryland Historic Press. 1994.

Roosevelt, Eleanor. *Tomorrow is Now.* New York: Harper & Row. 1963.

Rosebush, James S. *First Lady, Public Wife.* Lanham, MD: Madison Books. 1987.

Skarmeas, Nancy. *First Ladies of The White House.* Nashville: Ideals Publications. 1995.

Suarez, J.C. and Beck, J. Spencer. *Uncommon Grace.* Charlottesville, VA: Thomasson-Grant. 1994

Summers, Anthony. *The Arrogance of Power.* New York: Penguin Putnam. 2000.

Thomas, Helen. *Front Row at The White House.* New York: Charles Scribner's Sons. 1999.

Truman, Margaret. *First Ladies.* New York: Random House. 1995.

Vidal, Gore. *The Golden Age.* New York: Random House. 2000.

West, J. B. *Upstairs at the White House.* New York: Coward, McCann & Geoghegan. 1973.

Zinn, Howard. *A Peoples History of the United States.* New York: HarperCollins. 1995.

CAMP DAVID DIARIES
ORDER FORM

The following titles can be ordered direct from the publisher or from your local bookstore as they become available. All titles are each $19.95. Please indicate the number of copies you would like of each title. Send your order with your check in the correct amount to the address below. Plan on collecting the entire series. Thank you.

The following titles are available now.

Quantity

_____	Volume 1	Anna Eleanor Roosevelt
_____	Volume 2	Elizabeth Wallace Truman
_____	Volume 3	Mamie Doud Eisenhower
_____	Volume 4	Jacqueline Bouvier Kennedy

Total   #_____ x
$19.95 $_____ +
6% Sales Tax   _____
Shipping $ 4.95
Total $_____ **Enclose Check for this amount**

The following titles can be ordered now and will be shipped when printed. (Do not send payment in advance for the titles listed below. You will be notified when available in 2002.)

_____	Volume 5	Lady Bird Johnson
_____	Volume 6	Pat Ryan Nixon
_____	Volume 7	Elizabeth Bloomer Ford
_____	Volume 8	Rosalynn Smith Carter
_____	Volume 9	Nancy Davis Reagan
_____	Volume 10	Barbara Pierce Bush
_____	Volume 11	Hillary Rodham Clinton

Mail Orders and Payments to:
STERLING-MILLER PUBLISHING Co. Inc.
12573 Woodmill Drive
Palm Beach Gardens, FL 33418

Send Comments and Suggestions to:
infact@southernet.net
561-775-0839 Fax

ISBN 0-931791-05-7